I MET A WITCH

BATTLING EVIL WITH HOLY SPIRIT POWER

By Rhonda Dippon

PublishAmerica
Baltimore

First printing

Names of most of the people in this book have been changed to protect identities.

All Scripture quotes are taken from the Holy Bible, New International Version ®, copyright ©, 1973, 1978, 1984 by International Bible Society. Used by permission of Zondervan Publishing House. All rights reserved.

ISBN: 1-4241-1135-8
PUBLISHED BY PUBLISHAMERICA, LLLP
www.publishamerica.com
Baltimore

Printed in the United States of America

To Cindy Urban

My partner in this story, my good friend, my sister in Christ.
I couldn't have done it without you.

Special Thanks to:

- Judy, my writing teacher who encouraged, edited and helped shape this book.
- The gang of editors—Bekah, Missy, Jill and Rachel—who pointed out all my bad writing mistakes. I needed you.
- My prayer group—Urbans, Harts, Gregorys, Picketts, Wyssmanns and Darrell. You kept my vision alive and prayed me through. What a blessing and encouragement you've all been to me.
- My husband and children who stuck through the turmoil of that time with me and came out wiser and stronger in Jesus because of it.

PREFACE

I love roller coasters, but I'm afraid of heights. This might sound like a dichotomy, but since a roller coaster goes fast and doesn't stop at the topmost height, then the ride becomes thrilling along with a bit of fright. One time, though, I was in the second car from the front with my husband when we stopped dead—right at the very crest of the largest peak. I don't know why it stopped, but there we were, stuck on the edge of the world. Some might enjoy the view from the top, but I began to panic. My heart raced and my knuckles turned white on the bar in front of me. I began babbling about getting off that thing, and Darrell put his arms around me to try to control my increasing fears. I had a moment of a barely controlled sense of wanting to jump out of that car in order to end the terror overwhelming me. Of course, I didn't jump out, and I did calm down as I closed my eyes and prayed. We were trapped up there for 20 minutes before we finally started the long fall downhill. Believe it or not, I still love roller coasters. I didn't get on any more that day—or that year, but the next year I rode them again with glee.

This story is much like that roller coaster ride. I loved doing the Lord's work—so long as I was safe and secure. But when times became difficult, even dangerous, I sometimes felt like bailing. I never did, however. I kept riding the roller coaster up and down every hill till the Lord stopped the ride. There were definitely some scary moments, but there were also some very thrilling times on that wild ride.

It all started in 1984, when I was busy being a wife, mom and Mary Kay consultant, going to church on Sunday and a ladies' Bible study on Wednesday. I knew absolutely nothing about witchcraft or the occult, but because I persevered through this experience, I am now knowledgeable about these subjects. I don't claim to be an expert; but if you are ignorant about witchcraft and the occult now, you won't be after you read this book.

This is my testimony about a four-month period of my life where I experienced the power of the Holy Spirit as I never had before. I did not seek out this experience, but I believe God chose me for the task. Why He picked me is still a mystery, yet I know that He sometimes selects the weak so that His strength is glorified rather than ours. My only "strength" was that I loved to tell others about Jesus, and that's what God started with. He uses whatever we yield to Him; then He begins the process of molding and shaping us into the finished product that He designed us to be.

I had underestimated my ability to be used by God, and I also found that I had unintentionally put God in a tiny box and had allowed Him only so much room to move in my life. He is much too big to fit in any little space that we might try to shove Him in, and He wants out. My prayer for you as you read this testimony is that you smash any boxes that you have created to fit yourself or God into, and ride that scary roller coaster through to the end.

Although this is my story, it's really about God. Although Satan and his demons are talked about in this book, God is the strongest character. May God be glorified in this book, and may He be glorified in and through you.

Chapter One
DIVINE APPOINTMENT

"You did not choose me, but I chose you to go and bear fruit—fruit that will last. Then the Father will give you whatever you ask in my name." John 15:16

"Do you believe in the power of Satan?" Tammy asked, looking up at me with timid, questioning eyes and sweet, angelic hopefulness. The question definitely did not fit the look I saw on her face.

What a strange question, I thought. I'd faced other tough questions when I'd witnessed before, but nobody had ever asked me that one. *How did I get here?* Smile fixed on my face, my mind spun like a whirlwind.

It all started in July when I had picked Tammy's name out of a jar at the Ramsey County Fair. I was a Mary Kay consultant, and my sales unit ran a booth at the Fair where people signed up to win prizes. We divvied up their names after the fair was over and then called up each prospect to offer the person, and hopefully a few guests, a free facial. When I telephoned Tammy, she said yes to a facial and said she would invite some friends, so I set a date for mid-September to do a beauty show for Tammy and whomever else she'd invited.

I'd almost opted out of the show altogether when I sat in my blue minivan peering at the four-story, red brick apartment building. The Selby-Dale area in St. Paul was notorious for being a "bad neighborhood" with drugs, theft and I'm not sure what else, but this particular block looked all right—not shabby and unkempt. I waited a few minutes to see what sort of people came through the big glass doors, just to make sure.

Last month I'd held a Mary Kay show that I should have skipped. The neighborhood there was run-down—weedy lawns needed mowing, and dilapidated houses needed repair and paint—just like the house I did the beauty show in. While I was in the kitchen with the women, there were several men hanging out in the living room. The loud arguing and foul language coming from the other room both frightened me and gave me the creeps, and I suspected they were smoking pot from the sweet, smoky smell wafting into the kitchen. I half expected to see slashed tires when I left or to be nabbed between the house and my car. Nothing happened, but I promised myself that I would never put myself in a situation like that again if I could help it.

So I was watching the apartments and the parking lot to assure myself that this would not be a dangerous place. I was looking for any sign of drunkenness, the smell of pot, rough-looking characters, yelling or swearing—anything that would make me feel unsafe. I still had the car running and the doors locked, and I was prepared to drive away from my appointment and be a no-show.

Soon a couple exited, dressed in jeans and talking quietly—no problem there. A car with two men in it pulled up a few slots away, and they didn't look like they were drug addicts or drunkards. So I decided this was not a dangerous situation, gathered my bags of cosmetics and headed for the glass doors. Since there was no security in the building, I stepped into the empty elevator and pushed the four button, Tammy's floor.

The elevator doors opened with a jerk. I proceeded into the hallway, heels clacking on the tile floor, and took a few deep breaths to calm myself—meeting new people was always two steps out of my comfort zone. I walked to the T, and then turned right, looking for 406; it was the last door on the left. I set down my bags, straightened my black skirt and red silk blouse, lifted my hand to knock, then smiled at the "Footprints" poem that was nailed to the outside of her door. *Ah, she's probably a Christian,* I thought. A little more at ease, I rapped on the door.

A plumpish young woman dressed in navy sweat pants and gray T-shirt and with her brown hair pulled back into a ponytail answered my knock. Even though my two-inch heels lifted me to 5'6", I was still at least an inch shorter than her. "Tammy?"

"You must be Rhonda," she smiled.

"I am. Are you ready for me to set up for your show?"

"Come on in." She opened the door and stepped back to give me room to enter with my wide load—a burgundy bag full of products hanging from each hand and a pink beauty case full of samples draped over my right shoulder.

Tammy's studio apartment was the smallest one I'd ever seen. Walking through the door planted me in the middle of her kitchen. About three steps further and I was in her dining area, which then emptied into the corner living room. Her bedroom was crammed into the third corner and was visible from the dining and living area. The only door within the apartment led to her bathroom, which was off the bedroom and behind the wall of the kitchen, completing the square. Though tiny and sparsely furnished, it was neat and clean. I also noticed a Christian plaque on the wall above the couch and a calendar with Bible verses on it hanging next to her refrigerator. Reassured and more comfortable, I began to set up my sample case on the nearby kitchen counter and the trays and mirrors on the chrome and white table.

Tammy was friendly, and we chatted easily while I prepared my beauty show for Tammy and her guests who would arrive shortly. She'd lived there about a year, and said she wasn't working at the moment because she was planning to go to a business college soon.

Her two friends slouched in together from their own apartments. Both were dressed in sweats like Tammy; the tall, heavy one had stringy blonde hair, the other was a shorter brunette. They shuffled in with barely a hello and plopped down at the kitchen table. *They seem strange.* Shoving that thought aside, I tried to engage them in a little small talk to get to know them, but Debbie and Cheryl weren't interested. In fact, they seemed as dull and lifeless as blobs of clay. They continually looked down at the table as they filled out the beauty questionnaires and even as I began to fill the depressions in their trays with my samples. When they did look up at me, I shivered and froze. The dollop of cleansing cream landed on the table instead of the tray.

It was their eyes. I'd never seen eyes so glazed and blank before.

Remembering my other recent experience, I tried not to panic. I'd seen glazed eyes there that seemed drugged out, and I'd seen dull eyes that belonged to a woman who was mentally handicapped. But these girls' eyes were different somehow. Glancing back and forth between the two of them, my eyes were drawn to theirs—bottomless chasms that hid an emptiness you could drown in, or that they'd already drowned in. They seemed like shells of women with nobody home behind the eyes. *These two are definitely odd.* I didn't have any other category for what I saw, so I opened up the file cabinet in my brain and placed them in my "Weird" folder. Then I securely shut that door, cleaned up my mess and focused my attention mainly on Tammy while trying to avoid those two sets of eyes.

When I talked about the company, I liked to repeat Mary Kay's credo for herself and her consultants: "God first, family second and career third." As a Christian, I'd asked God to use me as a witness in my business, and that was my way of introducing God into my shows. I'd never received any kind of response to this little spiel before, but I kept saying it at every show hoping someone would comment on it. I liked to crack open a window that would allow room for a response—that way talking about Jesus with people seemed easier and more natural for me.

I loved to tell people about Jesus when I had the chance. I grew up in an unchurched home and became a Christian as an adult after my boyfriend, now my husband, asked me to go to church with him. I knew what it was like being on the "other side" and had a heart for those who didn't know the good news about Jesus Christ. I unfurled my sentence about God at Tammy's show with no apparent reaction.

Usually a show lasts two hours, but I whipped through my whole presentation in sixty minutes, hoping to halt the creepy feeling that was crawling up my spine like ants on a slow march. I wanted to sweep something off me, but I knew there was nothing tangible to brush away. When Tammy's friends left at 8:30, I was relieved to see them go. The show was a dud—I sold nothing. But as I was cleaning up, Tammy asked a question.

"You mentioned God tonight. Are you a Christian?"

I perked up at this question. All along I'd been thinking that she was a Christian because she had Christian-themed items hanging on her walls. I thought this probably wasn't a witnessing opportunity, but I answered Tammy in a way that would keep the conversation going and hopefully draw her out. "Yes I am. Are you?"

"No," she hesitated. "Before I tell you what I am, can I ask you another question?"

15

"Sure," I said. I had no idea where this would lead, but I was always up for witnessing. Now it looked as though the evening was taking an interesting turn, and I was ready and eager. Sharing the good news of Jesus was a joy to me that I couldn't get enough of. God had finally answered my prayers to use me in my business for His glory.

Now Tammy had just asked me that weird question about Satan. I was zipping off silent prayers alternating between, *What am I doing here?* and *How do I answer that question?*

In fact, I knew nothing about Satan except that he is the one who tempts us. *Never mind Satan, I'll focus on Jesus. I know Jesus.*

With all the bravado I could muster, I said, "Yes, Tammy, I do believe that Satan is powerful. But I know someone who is more powerful than him."

"Who?"

"Jesus Christ."

I'd learned enough about witnessing to know that it's best to start with the person's own questions rather than some formulaic plan, so I started with the power of Jesus. Deciding that my clean-up could wait, I pulled a kitchen chair away from the matching table and sat down knee-to-knee facing Tammy.

I told her that Jesus is God's son, but He is both true God and true man sent to earth to save people from their rebelliousness towards God and His law. Then I talked about Adam and Eve disobeying God in the Garden of Eden, and how that caused all people to be born as sinners in need of a savior. I said that God is a merciful God who loves us very much, but He is also a just God who hates our sin.

"God must really hate me then, because I've done a lot of stuff." Tears began sliding down Tammy's cheeks. Clasping her hands together and jamming them between her knees, she scrunched her shoulders up and seemed to shrink into herself like an iris starting to wilt.

"No, Tammy. He doesn't hate you; He hates your stuff. That's why He sent Jesus. Jesus took the punishment for our sins so that we don't have to. Jesus died on the cross for our sins so that we don't have to die and go to hell. Jesus then rose from the dead, which means that when we die, we get to rise also and be with Jesus forever in heaven. Would you like to be with Jesus in heaven when you die, Tammy?"

Head bent and hunched forward, she nodded.

"Heaven is a free gift that God gives to us. We don't deserve it because we're sinners, but He offers it to us freely when we believe in Jesus Christ and trust Him for our salvation. Only Jesus can save us from our sin; we can't earn heaven on our own, and there's nothing we can do to save ourselves."

I placed my hand on her arm and bent forward to look into her eyes. I wasn't sure how much of this was getting through to her so I decided to tell her my testimony.

"Tammy, about twelve years ago I was not a Christian. I grew up occasionally going to church with a neighbor or a friend, but my family never went to church. We didn't pray, and we never talked about God. I knew nothing about God until my husband Darrell started taking me to church when we were dating. Then I went to a class where I learned more about Jesus—the same things I've shared with you tonight—and it made sense to me. So I placed my trust in Jesus after that class, and I've been a Christian ever since. Does what I told you tonight make sense to you Tammy?"

Nodding. "I've heard some of it before. My foster grandma was a Christian and she sent me to a Christian camp one summer when I was ten."

"Have you ever put your trust in Jesus Christ before and received Him as your personal Savior?"

"No."

"Would you like to do that now, with me?"

"How do I do that?"

"I can lead you in a prayer where you'll invite Jesus to come in and take over your life. You'll confess that you're a sinner, ask Him to forgive your sins and wash you clean; you'll accept Jesus as your personal Savior, then you'll thank Him for His gift of eternal life."

Tammy sat back, looked sideways and deflated as though I'd punched her in the stomach. "I've done a lot of stuff," she said.

"That's okay Tammy, I'd done stuff I was ashamed of too. You just confess it to Jesus."

She rolled her eyes and looked at me as though looking at a two-year-old who didn't realize that the stove was hot. "You don't understand. Remember when I asked you if you believed in the power of Satan?"

I nodded. I'd been so wrapped up in sharing the gospel that I'd actually forgotten the question I'd tossed aside like a dirty sock. Since I'd had no real teaching on this, Satan seemed distant and unreal. I'd never had to deal with him before, and I wasn't sure I wanted to now. The gap between my knowledge and reality was about to narrow, and it looked as though we were going down this dangerous mountain pass despite my fear of heights.

"Why did you ask me that question, Tammy?"

"I've been involved in the occult," she explained. Then she began to spew out the grisly story of how she got to where she was today.

She grew up on a farm in Wisconsin with her mom, dad, younger brother and sister. It was not the typical, happy, well-adjusted family that it appeared to be to the people in their small town. Both her father and mother were known as fine, upstanding members of their little community. Her brother and sister had no problems with Dad and Mom, but Tammy did. For years her father had abused her emotionally, sexually and physically.

Tammy stopped to let that information sink in. I felt at a loss for words. *What do you say to someone who's been abused?* I attempted to comfort her as best as I could, patting her arm and saying, "Tammy, I'm so sorry. What did your mother do about it?"

"My mom knew about it, but did nothing. She would even hurt me sometimes too, and she screamed at me and called me names. It wasn't always hitting, you know. Sometimes I'd sit at the supper table and be the last one served, and if the bowls got around to me empty, then I had to go to bed hungry. Sometimes they didn't even allow me to sit with them during dinner. I'd be locked out of the house until they finished, then allowed in to eat—if there was anything left. Occasionally I would be forced to sleep in the barn with the animals. One time my dad went after me with his gun, screaming that he was going to kill me. I got away and hid and slept in the barn that night. At least I felt safe in the barn. My dad never came into the barn at night." She looked searchingly at my face to see if I understood.

I nodded. My mind turned to her earlier mention of sexual abuse. Everything she told me made me ache for what she must have felt. I couldn't imagine growing up in a household like that.

"Anything else, Tammy?" I sat holding her hand and listening while she continued spilling more nuggets of information.

"My mother was involved in the occult. She had her friends over, and they'd have a séance, play the Ouija Board, do tarot card readings, palm readings, astrological charts; they'd look into crystal balls. Sometimes she invited me to participate, and I did."

Then Tammy's voice became softer and she smiled. "I had a foster grandmother who was a Christian. She loved me."

When she sent Tammy to a Christian camp as a child, Tammy experienced her first grand mal seizure. She said she still had seizures, but the doctors declared her to be healthy. She did not have epilepsy, nor was there any medical reason for her to be having seizures, but Tammy often ended up in the hospital because of her frequent bouts. She was on two different medications to stop the seizures, but Tammy hated taking the pills because they made her feel slow and sluggish.

She tried to tell others about her horrendous home life; but either they thought she was lying, or they did nothing to solve the problem. Teachers thought she was simply making up tall tales because her parents were so esteemed in the community. Finally when she was sixteen, a new teacher at her school believed her story and reported it to Social Services.

Tammy was removed from her home and placed in a foster home for a little while. Her social worker, Jan, spent a lot of time with her and tried to help her during this difficult period. After a while, Jan told her that she knew what Tammy needed. She needed Satan. Satan would help her get over what her parents had done to her.

Jan was a witch who was a member of a coven—usually a group of thirteen witches—and she began to get Tammy involved in witchcraft. She would invite Tammy to social meetings with other witches so that they would eventually become friends. Then she would include her in rites where the witches worshiped, performed séances, gazed at crystal balls, levitated and participated in other occult practices. Much of what she experienced with Jan was familiar to her because her mother practiced these same rituals. With Jan as her mentor, she became immersed in her new lifestyle and new friends.

Tammy was later returned to her parents' home again for a time, but the situation didn't improve. A year before I met her she decided to move to St. Paul to get away from her family and start over in a new place. Jan helped her find the apartment she now lived in, and she still called and visited her occasionally. She even introduced her to her two new friends, Debbie and Cheryl, who were witches also.

So that's why their eyes looked weird. I wonder why Tammy's don't look like theirs? I looked again into Tammy's eyes—hers just weren't like Debbie's and Cheryl's.

I leaned back in my chair and let out a long breath. I was shocked by Tammy's story. It was almost too much to take in all at once, and my mind swirled in an eddy of emotions that threatened to draw me down into a dark drain.

Even though I was only 31 and not much older than Tammy, my maternal instincts took over with feelings of compassion for her and anger towards her parents and Jan. The fact that a social worker could get someone involved in witchcraft was both appalling and repulsive. I boiled inside at the idea of Jan turning an unknown number of young people towards witchcraft. This woman had abused Tammy just as her parents had. My eyes pooled with pity for Tammy because of all she had been through, and I wanted to protect her from further harm somehow. This wild tale confronted my tame, sheltered life and demanded attention. But I had no place to put it.

Although I was vaguely familiar with some occult practices, I never thought witches were real. *Weren't they make-believe—complete with black pointy hats, black dresses or capes and warts on noses? Weren't they wicked, evil, fantasy people with long, sharp nails and cackling laughs?* Now I had a witch sitting opposite me. And I was holding her hand.

And Satan. He was real, but distant. *Wasn't he over there somewhere in someone else's dark corner? Wasn't he behind all the evil in the world—like drugs, and abuse ...and witchcraft?* Suddenly Tammy's square studio apartment seemed even smaller; I felt boxed in.

I had to invent a new folder in my mind labeled "Occult" in order to have a place for all this new information I was learning.

21

I knew that I was deep into territory that was dark and unfamiliar, but I was the only person there in the apartment with Tammy. So I forged ahead and clung even more fiercely to the fact that Jesus was more powerful than Satan.

"Wow! Most of what you told me is totally new to me, Tammy. But I know that God can forgive any sin; there is no sin too big that He can't or won't forgive. We can just pray that He will forgive your sin of involvement in the occult. But He also wants you to forgive others. Do you think that you can forgive Jan for getting you involved, your brother and sister for ignoring the abuse and even your mom and dad?"

"I don't know if I can forgive my dad." She shook her head and looked away.

We talked about forgiveness for awhile, and then she decided she was ready to pray. I led her in a prayer where she asked Jesus to forgive her and then placed her trust in Jesus as her Lord and Savior. I welcomed her with a hug into God's kingdom as a new sister in Christ, and then we prayed again. She forgave Jan, her brother and sister, her mom and even her dad. She was sobbing by the end of the prayer, and it took her awhile to compose herself. She blew her nose and sat slumped in the kitchen chair, exhausted, but smiling. It was time for me to leave.

I encouraged Tammy to read the gospel of John—her foster grandmother had given her a Bible—and to pray every time she needed God's help. And I gave her my phone number so that she could contact me any time she needed to.

I left her that night about 10:30. This conversation had taken two hours, but I didn't mind the time; I was exhilarated! *Imagine the chances of my getting Tammy's name rather than someone else in my unit. Imagine the chances of her saying yes to a show, of her friends leaving so early, of Tammy picking up on my God spiel. That's a lot of coincidences. Maybe God set the whole thing up.* That was a new thought. I didn't remember anybody ever talking about how God could make everything fall into place when He wanted a person to be His witness. *Maybe there are no coincidences.* I remembered wondering what I was doing there earlier; now I knew why I'd stepped into that apartment, into Tammy's life.

I told Tammy that I would call her tomorrow, and we'd talk about going to church. I walked out to my car naively knowing that Tammy would need discipling, but I had no idea just how much God would be asking of me in the months to come. I wasn't as ignorant as when I'd walked into Tammy's apartment, but I still didn't understand what to do with it all.

My witnessing to Tammy had set the spiritual world into motion, and I could neither see nor discern its activity. I'd hacked into an unseen nest of hornets, and was blithely striding away oblivious to the swarming agitation. Some were frantically trying to repair their butchered nest, while others were gathering for the attack. Tammy would be the first target, but it would only be a couple weeks before I felt the initial sting.

Chapter Two

REINFORCEMENTS

...he sent them out two by two and gave them authority over evil spirits.
Mark 6:7b

I plopped all my bags on the floor in the back of my minivan and started off toward home. It seemed as though I were driving seven feet above the street—I was so exhilarated from my witnessing experience with Tammy. Homes, churches, playgrounds, stores—all blurred into one gray smudge as I passed by. With adrenaline pumping like a basketball player who'd just scored the winning shot, I worked my way up Dale Street into suburbia. Somehow I focused enough of my attention on my driving so that I didn't have an accident on the way home. Usually I hated driving at night, but I barely noticed the darkness.

I said a quick prayer for Tammy and thanked God for the opportunity to be used by Him.

"I should tell Gretchen!" I said out loud to no one. She was my sales director and also a Christian. I knew she would enjoy hearing about Tammy.

Just then a new thought flew into my brain like a missile. "Of course, I should tell Cindy!" I said aloud, striking my steering wheel. *She'll be absolutely thrilled to hear about Tammy. Maybe she'd like to help me with her.*

Cindy and I had been in the Evangelism Explosion program together a couple years ago, and last year we'd taught 7th and 8th grade Sunday School together at our church. Through teaching together, we'd become friends, and I knew how much Cindy loved the Lord and enjoyed talking about Jesus with anybody who'd listen. It made perfect sense to tell Cindy first.

Suddenly I realized that the thought hadn't been my own. It had been God.

I never heard a voice, but I knew it was God who'd given me the idea to call Cindy. Awe overwhelmed me and heightened my urgency and excitement. His presence had never seemed so near to me before.

I pulled up into my garage and hopped out of the car, slamming the door. Sliding open the van's back door, I lugged my bags out and drug them into the house. In the entryway, I dropped everything and pounded up the stairs forgetting that it was late and everyone was in bed already. My three children would be asleep downstairs in their two bedrooms, while my husband would be in our upstairs bedroom since the living room was dark. I decided to talk to Darrell first, then call Cindy. *Maybe he isn't quite asleep yet.*

I crept into the bedroom and found Darrell still reading by the light in the headboard cupboard of our waterbed. "You're later than normal," he said.

"I had the greatest experience! I shared Jesus with the girl who hosted the show tonight. We prayed for her to receive Jesus as her Savior." I gave him the short version of the story and told him why I just had to call Cindy that night.

"Maybe you should wait till morning to call Cindy. She could be in bed already; it's late, you know."

"Cindy won't mind. I have to call her tonight. I don't think I can sleep until I tell her."

"Well, talk quietly then. You don't want to wake up the kids."

"I will." Giving him a quick kiss, I noiselessly shut the door behind me and felt my way along the wall in the hallway and into the kitchen. Flipping on the light and grabbing the phone, I dialed Cindy's number and paced impatiently while it rang. Hoping Cindy would answer rather than her husband Bruce, I was relieved when a groggy female voice responded on the other end.

"Cindy! Did I wake you?"

"Yes. Rhonda? What time is it?"

"It's after 11. I'm sorry I woke you, but get out of bed; you've got to hear this. You're going to be thrilled; I just know you're going to love this."

I splashed the whole story out in a 15-minute gush with only a few spurts of single words from Cindy. "Well, what do you think? Will you help me disciple her?"

Cindy let out a surge of air. "Wow. Of course. Of course I'll help. This is exactly what we're supposed to be doing—witnessing to others. But I don't know anything about witchcraft or the occult."

"Neither do I, but that doesn't matter."

"I should know something, though, after all the Christian schools I went to. But I can't think of any teaching on this."

"Well, we'll learn together. Now, what do you think we should do next?"

We discussed our plan of action. Getting Tammy to church on Sunday seemed like the first logical step. Unfortunately, I was going out of town on Saturday, flying to Indiana for a week to take care of my mother after her hospital stay. It would be up to Cindy to get her there.

My part of the strategy would be to check in with Tammy

tomorrow to see if there was anything I could do for her and to tell her about Cindy. Then Cindy would follow up by calling her on Saturday to make arrangements for picking her up and driving her to church on Sunday. That determined, we said our good-byes and wished each other good luck in getting to sleep that night.

I quietly undressed and washed my face before slipping into bed. Then I lay there reliving the whole event. Even though the abuse and occult aspects of her story left me feeling like I was neck-deep in a river with a swift undercurrent, the fact that she'd turned her life over to Jesus was the sparkling, rippling surface water that I dwelled on till I finally fell asleep.

The next day, Friday, I called Tammy from my kitchen phone while my youngest, Rachel, played with her lunch at the table. My older two children, Derek and Dawn, were at school. Tammy said she was fine, and she sounded cheerful. She thanked me for spending so much time talking with her the night before. I told her how exciting it had been for me to tell her about Jesus. She chuckled at my bliss; I don't think she understood the enormity of her decision yet. I remembered back to when I'd accepted the Lord and how my future mother-in-law was so thrilled at my baptism. Meanwhile, I'd wondered what the big deal was. I figured that just as I had, Tammy would soon grasp the magnitude of praying to receive Jesus as her Savior.

I informed her that I would be going out of town tomorrow, but that I wanted her to have someone who was a Christian to talk to. "Do you mind if a friend of mine calls you tomorrow?"

Tammy hesitated, "I guess not. Does she know about me?"

"I shared your story with her and told her about your prayer last night. Is that okay?" I asked as I wiped up Rachel's spilled milk.

Tammy let out a sigh, "Yeah, then I don't have to tell it all over again."

"She'd love to pick you up on Sunday and take you to church. Would you like that?"

Tammy agreed to that suggestion but wanted to talk to Cindy first. So I called Cindy to let her know of my conversation with Tammy, gave her Tammy's phone number and told her I'd be back late afternoon next Saturday. Cindy would try to reach Tammy tomorrow.

On Saturday morning, Cindy tried calling Tammy several times in between household chores, but she had no answer. *I wonder where she is,* she thought as she was vacuuming the living room. God gently plopped a reminder into Cindy's thoughts about what I'd told her about Tammy and her seizures. Tammy had said that sometimes she would have a seizure outside of her apartment and whoever found her would call 911, and she'd be rushed to the hospital. *What if that's what happened to her?*

Cindy tried calling several more times that afternoon with no answer, but as she was washing dishes, she trusted that reminder about the hospital and turned to her husband Bruce as he came through the kitchen on his way outside. "Which hospital would a person go to if they lived in the Selby-Dale area?"

"Probably St. Paul Ramsey."

A few minutes later a receptionist answered after the first ring, "St. Paul Ramsey."

Cindy gave her Tammy's name and waited while the receptionist checked the computer to see if Tammy had been admitted.

"No. Sorry, nobody by that name has been admitted. Maybe she went to some other hospital," she said.

"All right, thanks," said Cindy.

"Well, wait a minute. If she came into the emergency room, she wouldn't be on the admit list yet. Let me check."

More waiting. "Yes, she's here in the emergency room, but it doesn't look as though she'll be staying overnight."

Cindy thought about her options as she dried and put away her dishes. Visiting a stranger in an emergency room didn't seem like the best idea, so she decided to try calling Tammy later that evening at her apartment. It didn't look as though Tammy would be going to church with her tomorrow.

About 9:00 that evening, Cindy dialed Tammy's number one last time before giving up for the day; Tammy still wasn't home. Cindy was disappointed that step one in our strategy for discipling Tammy had fallen through, but there was nothing she could do about it except pray for Tammy. *Lord, I pray that Tammy will be healthy enough to be released from the hospital tonight. I pray that she'll get a good night's rest in her own bed and that I'll be able to visit with her tomorrow.*

After attending the early church service with Bruce and their two children, Cindy telephoned Tammy late that morning while she removed sandwich fixings from the refrigerator for her family's lunch. Tammy answered the phone with slurred speech, and she seemed confused. It took a while for her to grasp who Cindy was, and Cindy began to speculate about this young woman on the other end of the line. *I wonder if she always sounds like this—so muddled and slow. Maybe she's just not well enough for me to see her today.* But finally Tammy livened up and seemed pleased with Cindy's suggestion to come for a visit that afternoon.

Cindy wiped the table clean after lunch and grabbed her jacket off the hook behind the door to the basement. As she was saying good-bye to her five-year-old daughter Keri, she felt an urge to take her along. "Bruce, do you think it'll be all right if I take Keri with me to Tammy's?"

"Sure, why wouldn't it be all right?" he asked from the living room floor where he was playing catch with their three-year-old son, Timmy.

"Well, because Rhonda told me that Tammy's been involved in witchcraft, and I'm not sure about that end of it."

"Don't take her then if you're worried about it."

"But the Church is always commanding us to tell others about Jesus. I grew up hearing that all the time, but I never heard an adult actually do it. This would be a good time for Keri to hear someone sharing Jesus, don't you think?"

Bruce sighed, "Cindy, I think you need to decide what's most important to you. If you're worried, then leave her here. If you want her to hear you witness to Tammy, then go ahead and take her."

"Keri, let's get your coat on. You want to come with Mommy to visit a nice lady and talk about Jesus?" Keri eagerly got ready; they trooped outside to their car and headed for Tammy's apartment.

As Cindy and Keri got off the elevator on the fourth floor and turned down Tammy's hallway, they saw a young woman standing in her doorway. Wondering if this was Tammy, Cindy paused at a voice she "heard" deep inside her. *Wait a minute. Put your guard up. Something's not right.* It was very subtle. She turned her head as though looking for the voice, but the hall was empty behind her. *Was that really God? What does He mean?* She'd had no sense of warning about visiting Tammy until now, and she didn't quite know whether to run or continue down the hall to meet Tammy. Still wondering why she should put her guard up and how exactly she was supposed to do that, she held even more tightly to her daughter's hand.

The young woman waved. *That must be Tammy.* Cindy felt hedged in with no perfect choice in front of her. If she went ahead to Tammy's apartment, what would she find that would compel her to put her guard up? But if she turned back to the elevators, how could she ever explain her actions to Tammy later? She pushed the tenuous warning aside, and she and Keri marched down the hallway to meet her.

Cindy and Tammy stood eye to eye, but Tammy outweighed Cindy by some 40-50 pounds. Tammy's face was crinkled in a girlish smile as she invited them in. Cindy and Keri took off their jackets in the kitchen and placed them over the backs of the chrome chairs.

After introductions, Cindy placed her hand on Tammy's arm and said, "Tammy, I just want you to know how thrilled I was to hear that you accepted Jesus as your Savior. You should know that you did the right thing and that Rhonda and I will be here to help you as you learn more about Jesus. I want to encourage you in your faith in any way that I can. If you have questions or need to talk about anything, I want to be there for you.

"Okay," Tammy answered shyly. She didn't quite know how to answer Cindy's encouraging words. "You want to come and sit down?"

Turning towards the living room, Cindy gawked at an array of paraphernalia spread out like a grotesque feast on Tammy's coffee table in front of her brown couch. There was a Ouija Board, which Cindy recognized, a pile of papers, some jewelry and candles. The candles were not anything Cindy would ever buy. There were red, black and gold taper candles and a red witch-shaped candle complete with pointy hat. The most evil-looking item on the table was a repulsive gold skull head. Keri pointed at it and asked, "Ooh, what's that, Mommy?"

Now Cindy understood the warning, and she didn't know how to answer her 5-year-old. She'd never seen this kind of stuff before, and it made her feel uneasy. Tammy led them to the couch and they all stared at the table full of occult objects before them.

The room felt vaguely dark and sinister like an unseen form hovered over the objects.

Keri reached out to pick up the skull. "Don't touch anything, honey," Cindy said, pulling Keri's hand back and holding onto her protectively.

"No, it's okay if she looks at it," said Tammy.

That was the last thing Cindy wanted Keri to do. "I'd rather she didn't."

Cindy scooted towards the far end of the couch away from the table and drew Keri up on her lap trying to distract her. Clearly this wasn't the nice little witnessing visit that she'd planned on. She remembered her conversation with Bruce and wished she'd opted not to bring her daughter into the midst of this dreadful display before them. *What was I thinking?*

The thought of Keri playing with any of the things laid out on the table made her stomach a tightly clenched fist. It all seemed so ugly and dirty in contrast to her pure motive of wanting Keri to hear her talk about Jesus. Her mind began sifting through ways to bring the conversation around to Jesus, but the banquet of horrid items before them demanded attention.

"What is all this, Tammy?"

Tammy explained that she'd received everything on the table in a box the day before. Jan, the witch who'd gotten her involved in the occult, had enrolled her in a witchcraft school—Wicca. "Every month I get a new package in the mail with lessons that I'm supposed to complete." She lifted up a packet of papers and thumbed through it showing Cindy the astrological charts, palm reading charts and lessons with questions.

"Hold it. There's a school where you can learn to become a witch?"

"Yeah. I'm doing it by mail; when I'm done, I'll be a certified witch. I get my box, read all the material, complete the lesson and send it back to them—I get to keep the other stuff. They grade my papers, then send me the next lesson and whatever else I need in another box. They send me things that are used in rites or for fortune telling or séances and things that help you in your life."

She picked up the necklace and matching ring. They each had a cheap-looking, tan-veined stone set in fake gold. "These are sort of good luck charms, or I could wear them during a séance to keep me safe from spirits that might want to hurt me. And you can have all your questions answered by using the Ouija Board. I like to play the Ouija Board."

Cindy remembered having a Ouija Board when she was a child and trying it out with her sister. "Wicca sent you the Ouija Board? Is this a witchcraft game?"

"Well, I guess so. My mom always had one when I was growing up. We used it all the time, asking it questions about the future."

"So, does it really work? I had one as a kid and that triangle thing didn't move when my sister and I put our hands on it, but it's supposed to move by itself, isn't it?"

"Mom always told me the spirits made it move, and Jan said that it's one way to talk to Satan."

This revelation put a new spin on that game that Cindy had never considered before, and she suddenly felt soiled because she'd played with the board as a child. She saw the game through new eyes; it was evil, a tool of witchcraft and of the devil. And the way Tammy ran her hand over the box and gazed almost lovingly at it made her flesh crawl like an infestation of termites scrambling over their next meal.

"I never thought of it in quite that way before," Cindy said quietly.

"Do you and Keri want to try it with me?" Tammy asked as she started to lift the top off the box.

Cindy put her hand over Tammy's to stop her. "No, that's not a good idea. What about the skull, Tammy?" She wanted to redirect Tammy's attention, but there was nothing good to divert it to.

Tammy picked up the hideous skull and explained that it was used in rites or for worship. The skull was painted gold and sat on a base that had what looked like Latin words on it, but Tammy wasn't sure what they meant. The base had a hole on either side of the skull where she inserted two black candles to demonstrate. The skull itself was about the size of a typical palm. Tammy cupped her palm over the head and petted it as though she were giving it a head massage. "You can either rub the head or light it up by placing a short candle here on top of the skull. Do you want me to light the candles?"

"No!" *Just what I need my daughter to see—some kind of witch rite,* Cindy thought. *Hold it. Did I just see flames in Tammy's eyes? No, my imagination must be getting the better of me.* She tried to look into Tammy's eyes again. *They do look like flames!* Tammy's eyes looked as though tiny flames were flickering deep inside the pupils giving them an eerie orange-red glow. Trying not to freak out, she looked away, fidgeted with Keri's blonde ponytail, tightening the pink ribbon. She took a deep breath and prayed silently, *Lord, help me.* Gazing into Tammy's eyes again, she saw that the flames had disappeared, and she let out the breath that she'd been holding. *Thank you, Lord.*

Clearing her throat, Cindy asked, "What are you going to do with all this, Tammy?"

"I think I should throw it away now, but I wanted you to see it first. Do you think I should wait and let Rhonda see it too?"

"No. I think you should get rid of it before then. I can tell Rhonda about it when she comes back."

"Okay. I'll throw it in the dumpster then."

34

"That's a good idea," said Cindy.

Cindy moved to the kitchen table so her back would be to the living room and put Keri on a chair next to her. "Do you mind if we sit here and talk?" She wanted to drag Keri's eyes away from the articles on the coffee table, and she was hoping her own guard was up sufficiently to block the darkness that surrounded the stuff behind them. She unconsciously ran her hand through her dark, curly hair trying to remove a creepy feeling like black spiders picking their way along her scalp.

Tammy offered Keri a Popsicle, and the two of them chatted a little while before they got down to the aim of the visit. Then Cindy began to talk about Jesus. Tammy pulled one of her several Bibles that she had in different translations off the makeshift bookshelf next to the couch. Cindy opened to the book of John and shared some very basic information about the life and purpose of Jesus. She explained that Jesus was God by pointing to passages in John 1, then turned to chapter four and showed Tammy where Jesus said He was the Messiah. Cindy listed some of the miracles that Jesus performed so that the people would believe. Then she flipped to chapters 19 and 20 and told her about Jesus' crucifixion and resurrection.

Tammy was a dry sponge soaking up Cindy's words like water. She asked a few questions along the way, and seemed to grasp the fundamentals of what Cindy was trying to share with her. It was an easy-going Bible study that helped Tammy feel comfortable with her Bible. Cindy suggested that Tammy should start at John 1 and read about Jesus for herself, then they could talk about any questions Tammy might have later.

Cindy asked Tammy about her hospital stay in the emergency room. She told Cindy that she'd had a seizure in the hallway by the elevator, and somebody from the building found her and called 911.

"I wish they wouldn't do that. I don't need to go to the

hospital. They should just leave me. I'm always okay after it's over—I just sleep it off. Now I have a hospital bill to pay." She did find out that her potassium level was very low, and was instructed how to eat more healthfully. "I have to be a monkey and eat bananas," she laughed, pointing to a bunch on the counter.

"Would you like to try to go to church again next week? Either Rhonda or I can pick you up."

"Sure. When's Rhonda coming back?"

"This Saturday. I'll telephone you sometime this week, but here's my number so you can call me if you have any questions or need me for anything, okay?"

As Cindy and Keri were walking out the door, Cindy remembered all the occult paraphernalia still displayed on the coffee table. Its evil presence irritated her. She turned to face it; the assortment looked as though it belonged there somehow, as though Tammy would turn to it for her next lesson right after Cindy walked out the door. She knew it should all be thrown out as soon as possible, but debated with herself about who should do it.

Tapping her nails on the doorframe and hesitating, she asked, "You are going to throw that stuff away, aren't you?"

"Yes, I will. I'll pack it up today and get rid of it. There are some other things I should get rid of too."

I wonder if I should offer to throw it away for her. No, it's better if she does it herself, Cindy thought. "Okay, but you should try to do it sometime today, Tammy. I'll talk to you in a few days."

If she'd known how difficult it would be for Tammy to throw out her occult collection by herself, she would have done it for her then. Cindy and I found out the word "occult" means "hidden," and all that junk would show up in hidden places in her apartment a week later. Everything on that coffee table was a snare for Tammy during the following days, trapping her in a vise that dug in and wouldn't let go, and pulling her back into the darkness.

The spiritual attachment between those objects and Tammy was evident when she'd seen the flames in Tammy's eyes as Tammy had massaged the skull. But she didn't realize the battle that was beginning to rage within and around Tammy, a battle that would be fought over Tammy's soul. Satan's kingdom had been robbed, and he wanted her back. He was ready to fight for what had belonged to him.

Chapter Three
PREPARED FOR BATTLE

When Jesus had called the Twelve together, He gave them power and authority to drive out all demons and to cure diseases, and He sent them out to preach the kingdom of God and to heal the sick.
Luke 9:1-2

"It's been an awful week," Tammy said on the phone. "I know you and Rhonda told me to read my Bible and pray, but I just can't." Tammy sounded as worn out and pathetic as a car that can barely turn over.

"Why not?" Cindy asked, stretching the long cord to check on her children playing in the back yard. It was Friday morning, almost a week since Cindy and Keri's visit.

"I bet I've had 50 seizures this week; I never have that many. Every time I tried to pray this week, I had a seizure. When I tried to read the Bible, I had a seizure. Then I couldn't read my Bible any more. It was too hot."

"What do you mean, your Bible's too hot?"

What on earth is she talking about? Cindy thought, plunking herself down at the round oak table in her kitchen.

"I'd pick it up, and it would be too hot to handle. It burned my hands, so I had to put it down. If I put it on the table to read it, then I'd end up in seizures."

"I've never heard of a Bible being too hot to handle. You don't mean that it literally burned your hands, do you?" Cindy asked, twisting the cord around her fingers. She was trying not to sound as though she didn't believe Tammy, but this seemed a little beyond strange—almost like an excuse a child would make up for not getting her homework done.

"No. But my hands did turn red. It felt so hot that I just had to put it down. So I really couldn't read much from the Bible this week."

Well, this is a new one. I guess I have to believe her. Why would she make something like this up? "Tammy, it's okay that you didn't read your Bible this week. I don't know what to do about it being too hot to handle, though. We can pray about that and about all the seizures you've been having too. Is it still okay if I come over tomorrow and bring my pastor and his wife? They'd love to meet you."

After her visit with Tammy last Saturday, she figured a couple more reinforcements couldn't hurt, so she called Pastor Ken and told him about Tammy. He was excited about meeting Tammy, and his wife Nancy agreed to come also. Since he said he'd prepare a simple Bible study for them all to look at while they were there, the pressure would be off Cindy to come up with something again. Cindy held a common view of pastors; she looked up from her lowly, ground-level square of sod to the sparkling white pedestal she'd positioned them on. Pastor Ken and Nancy had been on the mission field for fourteen years; surely they knew more about witchcraft and the occult than either Cindy or I did.

Besides, I was still out of town until Saturday afternoon, and Cindy didn't think it was a good idea to face the unknown alone. The last social call hadn't exactly turned out as she'd planned, and she didn't want to fly solo again in case there were more surprises.

"Sure, they can come with you; I don't mind. It's my birthday today, did you know that?"

"No, I didn't know. Happy birthday! How old are you? Are you going to celebrate?"

"I'm 23. A couple of my friends are coming over tonight, and they're bringing a cake."

"That sounds like fun." Cindy suddenly remembered that grotesque skull and other occult items and wondered if Tammy had thrown that stuff in the dumpster yet. "By the way Tammy, did you ever throw out that box full of occult stuff?"

"No. I haven't been able to do it yet."

"Why not?"

Tammy sighed, "Twice I was on my way out to the dumpster with the box, and both times I had a seizure. One time was in the elevator, and the other time was just outside my door. Both times, neighbors just dragged me back into my apartment, and the box came with me."

"When we come there tomorrow, maybe we should throw it all away for you. Okay? We'll see you tomorrow at 1:00 then."

After Cindy put her two children to bed that evening, she restlessly roamed the house looking for something, but she wasn't sure what, so she sat down at the piano and began to play in order to soothe her jittery nerves. But then she felt a nudging to read something from her Bible. Was it God? *I wonder where my Bible is? Probably on the basement bookshelf.* Picking her way down the basement steps, she stepped around boxes and stooped in front of the low bookshelf. Scanning the bindings of the books, she halted when her fingers hit the gold letters on black leather. Pulling it down off the shelf and dusting it off, she took it back upstairs, sat down and began flipping the pages. *What do you want me to read, Lord?* She started searching in Matthew, scrutinizing headings until her eyes caught "The Healing of Two Demon-possessed Men" in the eighth chapter. Instantly, she knew that God wanted her to read all the cases in the Gospels where Jesus called demons out of people.

You've got to be kidding me.

She stood up and paced the room, Bible in hand. If she read these accounts, then she would be saying that Tammy might be possessed by a demon—or demons. That idea was as foreign to her as the items on Tammy's coffee table. *I've never heard of anybody being possessed except in the Bible. Could this even happen any more?* Nobody talks about it—at least that she'd ever heard or been taught. Surely Tammy didn't have demons in her. She sighed and raked her hand through her hair. *Or did she?* Cindy remembered the Holy Spirit's warning that something wasn't right with Tammy and that she should keep her guard up. But what if Tammy was possessed?

A mental battle was being fought within her. If she did read the accounts in the Bible, then she might have to do what Jesus did—call out a demon. The thought terrified her. Her mind produced images of ghosts and unseen forces wreaking havoc and whooshing through Tammy's apartment, and she shuddered as though a frigid breeze was swirling through her own living room.

She ceased carving circles in her carpet. If she didn't read those passages, then she felt she would be disobeying what God desired from her. The idea of defying God brought a sense of panic like a child about ready to swipe a candy bar at the corner gas station. *Okay, God, I'll read my Bible.* She decided that reading the accounts from the Gospels would at least inform her about how Jesus took care of demons. So she sat down again on her rust-colored couch and opened her Bible.

Over the next hour, Cindy read every descriptive story that she could find in the four Gospels where Jesus drove out evil spirits. Jesus seemed to simply command them out saying, "Go," "Come out of him" or "I command you, come out of him." So that's what she'd do if she needed to—she'd command them out using Jesus' name. She noticed that where evil spirits appeared in the Bible, violence was also involved. Every case seemed to have the word "violent" somewhere in the story. But Jesus was never harmed by the demons, so she tried to swallow the fear that threatened to engulf her.

She read further that Jesus had given authority over evil spirits to His disciples, so she believed that, because she was a Christian, she must have that same authority. She'd been taught that all Christians could baptize somebody if there were no pastor around to do it, so she concluded that casting out demons would be similar. *There. Now I know what to do in case I need to do it.* Closing her Bible, she went to sleep that night satisfied that she had obeyed God.

The next morning, Saturday, Cindy did her normal house cleaning and then decided to run some errands. As she was standing on her stoop outside the side door to her house, she stared up at the sky. It was a normal Minnesota azure sky with a few wispy clouds scudding along the expanse. She felt compelled to look up but wasn't sure why; she saw nothing out of the ordinary, so she dismissed it from her mind and got into her car. When she locked her car to go into Snyder's Drug store, she turned and gazed up for a moment. Then coming out of Rainbow Foods, she stopped her cart to watch the sky. By the time she reached home, she realized that she'd caught herself peering heavenward for the fourth or fifth time that day. After greeting her family and putting away her purchases, she went outside and stood on her driveway and looked skyward to ask, "What do you want me to see, Lord?"

Although she saw nothing but sky with her physical eyes, her spiritual eyes watched a scene unfold in the heavenlies. She'd never had a spiritual vision before, but now God was painting a celestial picture for her. To her, everything she viewed was as real as the wind pushing the clouds. She observed Jesus in the air handing out equipment to His angels. These mighty warriors were strapping on armor, hefting swords, carrying shields. He gave to each one the war tool needed and gave orders to them about where they were going and when. Cindy "heard" God commanding them to be ready for battle in Tammy's apartment at 1:00.

Although the scene of warrior angels readying for battle was intense and overwhelming in magnitude, Cindy was not frightened, but calmed by what she was watching. She found herself nodding a silent agreement with God's actions. If what she'd read last night in her Bible actually happened this afternoon, she wanted those angels around her prepared for the battle. She thought, *You'd better show up because I'm going to need all the help I can get.*

The experience encouraged her spiritually, wiping away the gnawing fear that kept floating to the surface and threatened to spill over at the first sight of a demon. Freshly primed for what was to come, the spiritual vision gave her new confidence that she could handle anything that happened because God would be there with His holy angels.

On the way to Tammy's that afternoon, Cindy shared with Pastor Ken and his wife Nancy the conversation she'd had with Tammy the day before. They'd never heard of a hot Bible before, but Pastor Ken thought it was probably a demonic manifestation. This proclamation didn't help Cindy's nerves any. She didn't tell them about reading the Bible accounts about Jesus casting out demons, nor did she share her morning experience of the vision with them. Both encounters bordered on the bizarre, and Cindy wasn't ready to be thought of as an oddball. So she tucked them both just under the surface of her Lutheran Bible knowledge. But she brought her "sword" along with her this time—her Bible sat beside her on the seat, ready with marked passages.

Tammy greeted them all at the door. Bubbling over like a child who'd just opened her first Christmas present, she showed them the new canary that her friends bought her for her birthday. Perched quietly in the cage, the bird refused her coaxing to get it tweeting or singing. The cage sat atop its pole and stood between the living area and her bedroom. The whole time they were there it never peeped or chirped.

"It hasn't made a sound yet," Tammy said. "That's normal, I guess. My friends were told that it would take awhile for the bird to get used to its new home. Then it'll sing."

Looking into the cage, Cindy asked, "Who gave you the bird, Tammy?"

"Debbie and Cheryl came over last night with the bird and a cake."

"Are those the same friends that Rhonda met at your Mary Kay show?"

"Yeah, the same ones. Did she tell you about them?"

"Yes, she did." *Her witch friends. She's still seeing them. This is not good.* She was irritated and uneasy because Tammy had been partying with the two witches, but she also realized that Tammy had no other friends. Plus, the thought that those two had been in the apartment the night before caused her to take a quick searching look around the apartment to see if they'd left anything behind. However, she wasn't sure she'd recognize something that was occult in origin if she saw it.

They sat down in the living area; Cindy and Nancy settled on either side of Tammy on the brown couch, and Pastor brought a kitchen chair in and pulled it opposite them. He led them in a Bible study of sorts, talking about Paul's conversion in Acts 9. He seemed to be trying to make a connection between Paul's change of heart and Tammy's. But Tammy didn't know who Paul was, so Pastor Ken's discussion wafted somewhere over her head.

Although Tammy listened politely and nodded every now and then, Cindy could tell that nothing made any sense to her. She knew the Bible study was the apple at the top of the tree—out of reach. It wasn't really helping. What she needed was more basic teaching on Jesus, preferably from John since Cindy had started there last week.

Cindy fidgeted with the ribbon in her Bible, crossed and uncrossed her legs. The teacher in her was frustrated and antsy, but she didn't know how to help matters because this was her pastor whom she'd exalted to know-it-all status. Occasionally she interjected a few thoughts of her own to try to give Tammy something to grasp, but she knew that if she interrupted with her own teaching, it would be embarrassing to her pastor. So she let the Bible study pass by Tammy like so much smoke.

After they finished with the Bible study, Tammy told them about her many seizures that week and how the Bible felt too hot to touch. Pastor Ken said that they should pray about it.

Tammy rolled her eyes and moaned. "You don't understand. I can't pray."

"Why not?" asked Pastor Ken.

"Every time I pray, I end up having a seizure. Then I wake up on the floor two or three hours later."

Cindy put her arm around Tammy and held her hand. "This time nothing will happen to you. You'll be okay." Cindy was confident that Tammy wouldn't have a seizure with them there. Somehow she felt their Christian presence would arrest any demonic manifestations.

Nancy held Tammy's other hand, and they all took turns praying for a few minutes asking God to bless and comfort

Tammy and to stop the seizures so that Tammy could pray and read her Bible. They prayed that Tammy's Bible wouldn't be too hot for her, but nobody touched the Bible itself to pray over it. It was a fine prayer, but there were no commands, no mention of casting out demons. Then Pastor Ken and Nancy got up and donned their jackets. Cindy sensed an incompleteness to the whole afternoon but didn't know what else to say, so she slipped her coat on also. *Why did I read all those accounts in the Bible, and what was the equipment for if this is all there is?*

Cindy was the last one out the door, and as she turned to say goodbye, Tammy stumbled into the kitchen counter. She grabbed the door to steady herself, muttered a wobbly goodbye and closed the door.

Outside the door, Pastor and Nancy were already walking down the hall, but Cindy hesitated. Something wasn't right. She knew they weren't finished. Then she heard a sound coming from inside. "Wait a minute," she called. "I think something's wrong. I hear a noise."

Pastor and Nancy hurried back to the door, and they all leaned in and listened. Inside they heard a heavy, rhythmic clunking sound like something was hitting wood. Pastor straightened and backed away from the door, his face turning ashen. "I've heard of table tapping; I wonder if that's what she's doing. People who are in the occult take a cup or something, and they tap on a table. It's used to call up spirits for worship or a ritual."

Cindy's initial reaction was fear mixed with anger. "If she's in there calling up spirits after all we've done! We have to go in there."

Pastor and Nancy backed across the hall. "Go ahead," Pastor said.

Cindy knocked on the door and called Tammy's name. No answer, but the heavy clunking sound continued.

"Maybe the door's not locked. If it is, we'll have to get the landlord to let us in," Cindy said. They stood looking back and forth at one another. Cindy waited for Pastor Ken to take control of the situation, while he shifted his weight from one foot to another and looked down at the floor. Clearly she understood that he wasn't going to lead. Her pedestal thoughts about her pastor hung in the heavy air between them then slowly slipped into a palpable puddle on the floor.

She'd do it herself.

Cindy wavered with her hand on the knob. With thoughts of table tapping and calling up evil spirits in the back of her mind, she was afraid to go in. She had visions of horrible monsters with fangs and blood. Black things flying around the room. Long, sharp nails protruding out of hands attached to a witch dressed in black. Wispy, white, transparent ghosts. Hideous disembodied faces, mouths open in silent screams. Gripping fear. "Lord help me. If your angels are here, I need them now." Then she was reminded of a Bible verse from 1 John 4:4: "The one who is in you is greater than the one who is in the world."

She repeated this verse over and over in her mind until her faith was strengthened like pottery fired in the kiln, then she opened the door and poked her head in. Everything seemed just as they'd left it except for the continuing clunking. She entered as far as the living room, then spied Tammy sprawled on the floor in her bedroom.

"It's okay. You can come in," she called to the others.

They entered the living area and stopped at the sight before them in Tammy's bedroom. Tammy lay on the floor with her head between the bed and the dresser—the wooden noise was her head hitting the dresser rhythmically. Tammy was having a seizure. Her head thunked the dresser, her upper body vibrated, her arms were stiff and her breathing was erratic and labored.

They stood over her as though frozen to the tile floor, watching and doing nothing.

Cindy remembered her preparation for battle. She'd read those Bible passages the night before and discerned that this was the time to put what she'd learned into practice. But she couldn't do it. She didn't want her pastor and his wife to hear her. What if she was wrong? What if Tammy's seizure was epileptic and not demonic[1]?

The three of them looked at each other, but nobody budged. Again, Cindy knew that it was her move. She knelt down beside Tammy and placed her hand between Tammy's head and the dresser to stop the battering. Then she began to cry out of pity and compassion for Tammy. "Lord, what should we do? Please help her," she whispered.

Nothing happened. Cindy knew those weren't the words Jesus used, and she was disappointed in her timidity. She was supposed to give an order, not pray. Beating down the doubt that she was wrong and piercing a hole in her pride that felt too learned to command demons, she bolstered her courage, placed her hands on Tammy's shoulders and commanded quietly but firmly, "Out in the name of Jesus."

And the seizure stopped. Immediately.

Tammy's body quit vibrating; her head ceased its drum beat on the dresser, her arms relaxed, and her breathing normalized. Cindy sat back on her heels in amazement. *It's a miracle. I actually saw a miracle.* She was awestruck by the simplicity and magnitude of the act that took place at her knees. Peering heavenward in wonder, she remembered the warring angels. *Thank you, Lord.*

And this was the pivotal point in Cindy's spiritual life. From this moment forward her prayers would be uttered with more boldness and surety. The God of the Bible had come alive before her eyes. He truly was the same yesterday, today and forever. She needed the Lord to act right then, and He did. His authority was powerful. It's not that her prayers had never been answered before, but that they'd never been answered so instantaneously. The awesome power of Jesus' name had moved a mountain by stopping a seizure.

Cindy sat on the floor by Tammy and gaped in silent wonder. Pastor and Nancy were in the living room, but had heard her command and were as astonished by the result as Cindy was. This was a holy moment, and they were speechless.

Knowing that Tammy said she usually sleeps for two to three hours after a seizure, Cindy decided they couldn't wait. She wondered if she should push the door wide open and go for two answered prayers in a row. But her faith was reinforced, and she was ready to exercise it again like a shield in battle. "Lord, we've been here two hours already; we can't wait around another two hours. Wake her up, Lord."

Tammy began to move, and within ten minutes she was fully awake.

Twice in a row, God answered. He was no wimpy God who only had one miracle in Him. He was a bigger God than Cindy thought He was, and He could do anything. She saw that He not only could answer prayers immediately, but that He wanted to display His power to His people. He'd prepared her for the battle that He wanted to win—if she'd only participate.

"What happened?" Tammy croaked. "My head hurts. I had a seizure, didn't I?"

"Yes, Tammy. We heard a noise and came back in and found you having a seizure here on the floor. Your head was hitting the dresser," Cindy answered.

They camped around Tammy on the floor of her bedroom and began a nitty-gritty Bible study—this time focusing on Jesus. Cindy turned to John 10 to share Jesus as the good shepherd, then talked about Jesus as the true vine in John 15. Wanting Tammy to feel comforted, she ended with some verses from Jesus' prayer in chapter 17.

"Tammy, in this passage Jesus was praying to the Father for His disciples. He says, 'I pray for them. I am not praying for the world, but for those you have given me, for they are yours. Holy Father, protect them by the power of your name—the name you gave me.' That's the name of Jesus, Tammy. His name is powerful. 'My prayer is not that you take them out of the world but that you protect them from the evil one.' Jesus is asking the Father to protect those who believe in Him. Just so you know that He's not praying only for His disciples, it says, 'My prayer is not for them alone. I pray also for those who will believe in me through their message.' That's you, Tammy. Jesus was praying those things for you, too."

She assumed no knowledge on Tammy's part this time, keeping it simple enough for her to understand. But she didn't tell Tammy about the command she had spoken.

Maybe she wouldn't understand the enormity of it. Maybe they didn't either. Nobody detected demons flying out the window. But they viewed the violence of a seizure calmed by a command of authority in Jesus' name. Nobody noticed the angels with their equipment. But they beheld the battle halted and won—for now.

They saw a gentle answer to prayer that woke the slumbering spoils of war, and brought her back from darkness into the light.

Silently they traveled back to their suburban safety zone, battle weary, awed and shaken. Demons were real; they knew that now. And they thought the job was done. They forgot about the box full of occult paraphernalia that hid somewhere in Tammy's apartment. And no one understood that odious demons clung to those occult objects and to Tammy herself and wielded a power that would soon become apparent.

[1] Not all seizures are a medical disorder not to be confused with Tammy's problem. She did not have epilepsy; we believe her seizures were demonic manifestations..

Chapter Four
THE ONE WHO IS IN YOU

"You, dear children, are from God and have overcome them, because the one who is in you is greater than the one who is in the world."
1 John 4:4

"I can't believe you did that," I said in awe to Cindy, stretching the phone cord over to the stove to put the skillet down. I had just arrived home from Indiana that afternoon, and I only had an hour to prepare a sloppy-Joe dinner for friends who would arrive at 6:00 p.m. "I wish I'd been home earlier; I could have gone with you."

Cindy had phoned me immediately after arriving home from Tammy's apartment to tell me all about what had happened there. The command Cindy had uttered and the results were staggering news to me.

"I'm still reeling from it all. But at least now we know what we're dealing with," Cindy said.

"You mean that Tammy is possessed? Do you think she's still possessed, or do you think the demon is gone? What exactly are we saying here?" At least Cindy had been prepared for the news that Tammy might be possessed. Her Bible reading the night before and the morning vision of angels had primed her for the visit with Tammy. I'd just had the last twenty minutes to get used to the idea as Cindy spurted out the whole story. Wave after wave of new information beat on the shores of my mind. I had to have Cindy repeat herself in order to master these foreign ideas like *demon possession* and *calling out a demon*.

"I honestly don't know, but it seems to me that she's not done. Something still feels unfinished," Cindy said.

"So, Tammy might still be possessed, and I'm supposed to call her to tell her when I'm picking her up tomorrow for church?" I'd barely had time to unpack and greet my family. Now I was plunging back into a situation that I'd started, but that had suddenly become a lot more complicated. Sitting at my maple dining room table, phone in one hand and forehead pressed into the other, I was trying to block out the racket of three noisy children and concentrate on a story that seemed to have walked right out of the Bible and into my reality.

"I told Tammy to expect your call. She said she wanted to come to church with you. Are you okay? Should I pick her up? I can, you know."

"No, it's all right. I can do it. Darrell knows that we'd planned on picking her up tomorrow. I still think it's important for her to go to church—now more than ever, don't you?"

"Yes, I do. Since last time didn't work out, I hope that this time does. I'll be there at 9:30 to show Tammy around while you teach Sunday School, maybe introduce her to a few people. Then we can both sit by her in church," Cindy said.

"We'll stick with our plan, then. I'll call you if there's any problem, otherwise I'll see you tomorrow."

I hung up the phone, plunked into a chair and allowed myself a few minutes to let everything register in my brain. Initially I felt getting Tammy to church was a good discipling move. Tammy could meet other Christians, hear the Word preached, worship the Lord instead of Satan. Now the church-plan seemed weightier to me—more of a necessity and protection issue for Tammy. In God's House, I believed Tammy wouldn't have a seizure; she would be safe from Satan and his demons. This was all so radically new to me, and I felt inept, unqualified. But Cindy seemed to have survived the lion's den, so maybe I could muster enough courage to tackle whatever demonic activity that Satan might flaunt before me.

I dialed Tammy's number, but her line was busy. *I'll try again later.* I didn't have a lot of free time right then because I was expecting our friends, Stan and Emily, along with their two small boys in half an hour for dinner and cards. We usually got together once a month, and we hadn't cancelled even though I knew time would be tight between coming home from my trip and their arrival for dinner.

I called again right before our friends came, but the same monotonous beeping answered.

We had our supper with Emily's family and I cleaned up afterwards. Tammy's line was still busy. The kids all played downstairs with my older two children keeping order while we adults sat around the kitchen table playing euchre.

By 8:00 I still hadn't reached Tammy, and I was becoming worried. Cindy had told me about all the seizures Tammy had been experiencing, and I wondered if she'd had a seizure. I telephoned Cindy and relayed my problem so far. We decided that I should keep trying till 10:00.

At 10:00, *beep, beep, beep.* I decided to call the telephone company to see if I could find out any more information. They told me that her phone was off the hook. *Maybe she's lying on the floor by her dangling cord. Maybe she's just sleeping off a seizure. Maybe she's hurt.* Trying not to let my imagination escape into a spiraling tornado,

I called Cindy again. This time we had a more lengthy discussion about what to do. I would keep trying to phone Tammy.

I wasn't a very good hostess that night since my attention was half on our card game and half on Tammy, and every fifteen minutes I got up to place another phone call. My guests seemed to understand my agitation over the situation—at least they were polite about it anyway, but Darrell thought I should give up.

The last call was at 11:30—still no answer as I paced the kitchen floor.

The gentle nudging I'd felt from the Lord became a hard push—I should go down to Tammy's apartment to find out if she was okay or not. Activity was just what I needed to settle my fidgety worrying, so I didn't question this strategy that seemed to be coming from God. I announced my decision to Darrell, hoping he wouldn't think I was as irrational as I sounded to my own ears.

"You are not going down there alone," he said. "I'll go with you." I could tell that he wasn't exactly thrilled with my choice, but he was ready to back me up. He apologized to Stan and Emily about the way things had worked out that evening. "Do you guys mind staying here while we go down there?" All the children were in bed by now—ours in their own beds and theirs tucked into our waterbed.

"I'll go with you," Stan suggested. "Emily won't mind staying here with the kids, will you honey?" She agreed.

I breathed a sigh of relief. I was able to go check on Tammy, but I didn't have to do it alone; I was taking muscle.

On the trip down there, I silently rehearsed possibilities as I stared out the window watching the familiar scenery blur into an indistinct streak. *Maybe Tammy wasn't even home. Maybe she was in the hospital again. Or she could have injured herself in a seizure. She could be asleep with the phone off the hook. Or she could be dead.* Nothing seemed impossible any more, nothing too far-fetched.

One thing was sure. If Tammy was there, she was coming home with me. Getting her to church still seemed the ultimate goal, and I wasn't about to take any more chances. I was bringing her to church tomorrow no matter what. As the thought of bringing Tammy home with me embedded itself, I decided to keep it to myself. It seemed a little outside the "normal zone," but I was determined in my heart that it was the right thing to do. I glanced over at Darrell. *He's going to think I've lost it. Maybe she's not even there, so why bother him with my plan now*, I reasoned.

Flanked on both sides, I rang Tammy's doorbell. It was midnight by now.

I heard an immediate, "Who is it?" from inside.

"Tammy, it's me, Rhonda."

She opened the door garbed in her usual sweats and T-shirt. "Rhonda, what are you doing here?" She gave me a hug, but then backed off shyly when she caught sight of the two men with me.

"Tammy, this is my husband Darrell and our friend Stan. I tried to call you several times but kept getting a busy signal. I was worried about you when the phone company said your phone was off the hook." We came into the tiny kitchen and shut the door behind us. There was the culprit dangling to the floor from the wall between her kitchen and bedroom.

Tammy reached down to hang up the phone. "I forgot I left it off the hook," she said sheepishly. "After Cindy left today, Jan called. I told her all about what's been going on with me—that I accepted Jesus as my Savior, and that friends had just left after a Bible study. She was really angry with me. She started screaming and swearing at me, so I hung up on her. But she called back and started in again. I had a seizure, but when I woke up Jan was still on the line. I've never heard her so mad before. She's upset at you and Cindy too."

"You told her about me and Cindy? Does she know our names?" I asked. I didn't like the sound of this. I shuddered at the idea of Jan being aware of our identities. I had visions of her and her coven of witches circling in the woods chanting incantations against us.

"Yeah, I told her. She's not very happy. She said a lot of mean things and swore at me again. So I hung up. But she called me back later and tried to talk me out of being a Christian. She ended up screaming at me, and I had a seizure again. When I woke up, she was still yelling. I hung up again, but the phone kept ringing and ringing until I finally took it off the hook. I think I had another seizure after that. I don't know…"

The whole scenario with Jan brought me back to my earlier resolve in the van on the way there—Tammy should come home with me.

"Tammy, how would you like to spend the night at my house?" I didn't look at Darrell's face; I was sure it was a map of incredulity. "Why don't we pack a few things in a small bag; you can sleep over at my house tonight, and then we'll go to church together tomorrow. That way Jan can't bother you any more—at least not tonight or tomorrow morning." I looked over Tammy's shoulder at Darrell pleadingly.

He nodded and I sighed. He'd been so patient with my crazy ideas that I could have kissed him right then and there.

While the men waited in the kitchen, I helped Tammy pack a bag to take along. On the ride home, I sat in the middle seat of the van with Tammy while Stan occupied the front passenger seat. Recorded in the back of my mind was my phone call with Cindy, but I told myself that Tammy would not seizure at my house because it was a Christian home. *Satan wouldn't dare enter my house.* I buried the fear that threatened to rise up out of the pit onto solid ground. Tammy seemed so harmless as she snoozed against the window.

I thanked Stan and Emily profusely as they gathered up their sleeping children to leave. Stan thought it was an adventure. "It's not often that we get to meet a witch," he whispered conspiratorially. I was grateful that members of our church appeared to be embracing Tammy and our attempts to help her.

Tammy would sleep downstairs in the family room of our split-level house where Darrell was busy pulling the hide-a-bed from the gold couch. Meanwhile, I went to grab clean sheets and a blanket from the linen closet. Tammy stood in the center of the room, head bent, hands behind her back and her toe tracing the pattern in the green carpet. She wasn't used to all the fuss being made for her. "I can just sleep on the couch," she said.

"No, it'll only take five minutes to make up the bed, and you'll be more comfortable this way," I said. I showed her where the bathroom was, then I waited while she readied herself for bed. After seeing her safely nestled in bed and saying good night, I walked up the stairs to my own bedroom. I was glad that all the commotion had not awakened my own children whose bedrooms were just down the short hall from the family room.

"What time shall I wake you up tomorrow?" Darrell asked.

"Better make it 7:00. I may need the extra time, and I want everything to go smoothly."

It was after 1:00 by the time I slipped into bed next to my husband. I was exhausted, and it would be a short night.

I was still thinking that Tammy wouldn't seizure in my home, but just in case, I lay awake listening closely for any sound coming from downstairs. I heard nothing but the *tock, tock* of the pendulum on the cuckoo clock in the living room and Darrell breathing rhythmically next to me, so I comforted myself with the knowledge that everyone else was sleeping so I might as well try to get some rest also. The tension of the past few hours drained out of every muscle, and then my mind relaxed.

When the alarm went off at seven, I groaned. Still tired from the night before, I dragged myself out of bed and zipped into my lavender robe. Darrell showered while I woke up Tammy and our kids. I decided to wake Tammy up right away in case she wanted to shower. From my interactions with Tammy, I knew her to be rather slow moving and thought it would probably take her a while to get ready.

I walked down the stairs and rounded the corner into the family room and saw Tammy still sleeping. But before I reached the side of the bed, she began to have a seizure. Her upper body vibrated, neck and arms stiff. She seemed like a puppet whose invisible strings were being jerked up and down.

Cindy had described Tammy's seizures, but I'd never seen one before. It's one thing to hear about, but seeing it in person left me trembling as I leaned my hand against the wall for support. My fears mounted from my pounding heart to my pulsating temple. And I realized that Satan dared. He came right along with Tammy into my house and was causing her seizure in my family room. I took two steps backward, arms hugging myself. The sight before me was so frightening that I felt like racing up the stairs and out the front door to get away from it. But I only backed out of the room.

I felt like a guitar whose strings had all broken simultaneously. I sat down on the stairway to gather my jangled nerves somewhat, then went into my 12-year-old son Derek's room to wake him up. I told him we had a guest sleeping on the hide-a-bed and not to go in there. I busied myself picking out clothes for him that he was old enough to choose for himself.

You've got to go back out there and do what Cindy did. You heard what she said, and you know what to do, I admonished myself. *At least I won't have anyone to hear me do it.*

I collected my courage from the pit of my stomach, closed

Derek's door tightly and went back towards where Tammy still lay gripped in a seizure. She was now foaming at the mouth, and it was not a pretty sight. Covering my eyes momentarily, I repeated the same Bible verse that Cindy had told me she'd used outside Tammy's door to reinforce her own courage when she heard the thunking noise: "The one who is in you is greater than the one who is in the world." Since I'd never memorized many Scripture verses, I was thankful to Cindy for giving me this one. Sliding my hand down my face, I moved forward to stand over Tammy. From deep inside, dual reactions rose that layered over the fear like a blanket. I was both incensed at Satan and bolstered in the boldness of the Lord. Leaning over her and placing my hands on her shaking shoulders, I commanded, "You get out of her in Jesus' name!"

And she stopped. Her whole body went limp. *Whoa! Just like it happened with Cindy.* I realized that I had fully expected the same results that Cindy had had. I'd never even considered that Jesus' name would not have power over the demons, but it was stunning to see it in action. I stood over her for a few minutes before I decided she could sleep a little longer before trying to wake her.

So I turned and went into the girls' room to wake them and get their clothes laid out. I instructed Dawn, nine, and Rachel, four, the same as I'd told Derek, "Stay out of the family room." If ever I needed them to obey me, this was the time. They must have recognized my no-nonsense attitude because they all complied.

I went back down the hall to where Tammy slept and wham! She stiffened and vibrated again the moment I stepped by the bed. This time I only hesitated a moment before placing my hands on her shoulders and commanding, "Out, in the name of Jesus." Again, an immediate end to the seizure.

Back to the kids to help them get ready. The name plaques on their doors were like badges of protection: "Jesus loves Derek,

Jesus loves Dawn, Jesus loves Rachel." Tears blurred the declarations as I ran my fingers over the words and asked God to keep each of them safe. Their grandmother had no idea of the significance of those name plaques when she'd stuffed them in their stockings last Christmas. It was as if Jesus Himself stood guard outside my children's rooms.

Back to Tammy. As soon as I reached her, she began yet another attack. This was now becoming routine, so I simply repeated my earlier action and order with the same results.

One more time we both went through the ordeal. When I straightened up, I had an "aha" moment as I recognized the pattern. "The one who is in you is greater than the one who is in the world," I said out loud.

As a believer, the One who is in me—the Holy Spirit—is greater than the one who was in Tammy—an evil spirit or spirits. They were reacting to the Holy Spirit in me every time I entered the room. Tammy was paying for her involvement in witchcraft and the occult by being thrown into seizures. The evil spirits in Tammy tried to harm her just like the boy in the Bible whose father asked Jesus to heal him (Mark 9:14-27). The evil spirit often tried to injure the boy by throwing him into the water or fire during a seizure. Jesus healed the boy with one command; we'd ordered the demons out several times now, but still they persisted in causing Tammy's seizures. I had a deeper understanding of this demonic activity now, but I was still limited in my knowledge of how to deal with it.

Tammy was sleeping peacefully now, but I was still in my robe when Darrell came downstairs to see what was going on. I filled him in and then left him in charge while I went up to shower and get ready for church. I was glad that I'd risen earlier than normal that morning. By the time I came back down, the kids were all dressed and ready for breakfast, and Tammy was just waking up.

She was a bit worn out from her four seizures, but she clambered out of bed and went into the bathroom to get ready.

After we'd eaten our breakfast of coffee cake and orange juice, we piled into the minivan for the five-minute drive to church. Tammy was as cheery as a robin tweeting her first spring song as she talked with my children in the back seat.

Darrell took the kids to their Sunday School classrooms and went into the gym for his class. Tammy and I met Cindy inside the red double doors to the burgundy-bricked church. She'd been uncertain if Tammy would be there or not because I forgot to call her the night before because it was too late, and the morning had been too chaotic. Cindy was thrilled to see her and gave her a big hug. I had a brief aside to Cindy on the events of our morning, so she'd be warned of the possibility of more seizures.

After handing Tammy over to Cindy's care, I entered my classroom, the library off the narthex, where I taught 7th and 8th graders for the next hour. After my morning, I was a bit distracted, and it must have shown. One of the girls asked if I was all right. I took my time answering her. *No, I'm not all right, but how much do I tell them?* Deciding to share the bare minimum with my class of ten facing me in a semi-circle, I told them that I'd brought a young woman to church today whom I'd witnessed to just a week and a half ago. I also shared that she'd been involved in the occult and that we were finding out that the consequences were tough to deal with. I didn't want to divulge Tammy's past without her permission, nor did I want to give my students nightmares, but I was able to tie it all into the lesson for the day—idolatry.

Tammy's ordeal had given me an abundance of insight into the effect of that particular sin, and the lesson came alive both for me and for my students as it flowed out of my mouth. The authority and conviction of my teaching awed me. It was almost as if I was reading the God-inscribed ticker tape as it uncurled from my tongue. God's presence filled the small, book-lined room that Sunday as I stepped out of the way and allowed Him to teach those kids through me.

Meanwhile, Cindy took Tammy around the building and introduced her to people they met in the hallways. Our church had a school, kindergarten through eighth grade, that our children attended, and she found some artwork in the hallways that belonged to each of our kids. Cindy then took her into the offices where Tammy met a friend of ours, Laura, who was the kindergarten and pre-school teacher. Laura had been in the Evangelism Explosion program with Cindy and me, and we all happened to be the same age—31.

Often before Tammy was about to have a seizure, she'd have a physical warning signal—sometimes she felt woozy, or she'd smell a familiar odor or see an aura haloing before her eyes. Just fifteen minutes before the church service was to start, she warned Cindy that she thought she needed to lie down because she felt a seizure coming on. Laura knew where the cot was, and set it up in Pastor Ken's office where Tammy reclined and promptly did as she'd predicted. Cindy prayed over her and the attack stopped, but then Tammy slept. After I finished with Sunday School, I found them there in the office and took over the watch. I stayed with Tammy while Laura and Cindy went to church.

Tammy dozed the hour away, and I had plenty of time to ruminate. My naïve idea that Satan wouldn't dare step foot inside my church fizzled like a falling star. I wondered how many times Jesus' name would have to be invoked over Tammy. However, evidently demons don't like church services or sanctuaries, because this one only allowed Tammy inside the building, not into the service itself. Perhaps the sight of the large wrought-iron cross or the altar spread for communion caused the manifestation.

Just before noon Tammy woke up. After the service, there was a potluck which I wasn't originally planning to attend. We thought it would be a little overwhelming for Tammy to go to both church and a potluck, but since she'd slept through the service our plans now changed. Even though she was a bit shy, Tammy enjoyed meeting new people, and many went out of their way to be friendly towards her and talk to her. There was a small singing group that performed at the potluck, and Tammy soon had tears dribbling down her cheeks. Every song seemed to be sung just for her—particularly one about the prodigal son. Tammy's flushed cheeks dimpled through her tears as they played songs for everyone to join in, and she had no problem singing the Christian lyrics.

After the potluck Tammy asked Cindy, Laura and I if we'd help her clean out her apartment of all those occult objects that she still hadn't managed to get rid of by herself. After the songs she'd heard, she seemed to have a renewed interest in throwing out her Wiccan items. We decided that would be a good idea— that stuff needed trashing, and I had to take Tammy home anyway. And Laura was eager to come along even though she'd just met Tammy.

We told our husbands that we'd be back in two hours max— how long could it take, anyway? I'd already had an eventful, late evening followed by a chaotic morning that had left my energy level at half-empty, but I thought I could handle a couple more hours.

Forever afterward, the events of that afternoon would fall under the title of "That Sunday." If I said, "Remember that Sunday…" Cindy would immediately pull out this particular afternoon from all the other Sunday afternoons of memory. It would be permanently freeze-framed in both of our minds.

We found out that we'd only seen the foothills of the occult so far; the top of the mountain was roiling in clouds that were about to part. Battle lines were being drawn, and the fight for Tammy's soul was about to begin in earnest.

Chapter Five

THAT SUNDAY

Finally, be strong in the Lord and in his mighty power. Put on the full armor of God so that you can take your stand against the devil's schemes. For our struggle is not against flesh and blood, but against the rulers, against the authorities, against the powers of this dark world and against the spiritual forces of evil in the heavenly realms. Therefore put on the full armor of God, so that when the day of evil comes, you may be able to stand your ground, and after you have done everything, to stand.
Ephesians 6:10-14

I ran my family home in the van after the potluck, then pulled up in the circular drive in front of our church to pick up Tammy, Cindy and Laura. They piled in with Cindy and Tammy in the middle seat of the van and Laura in the front passenger seat beside me. I drove the familiar twenty-minute route down Dale Street to Tammy's apartment to help her trash her occult paraphernalia since she'd been unable to do it on her own. Tammy's demeanor started out smiley and perky as she prattled on about the fun she'd had at the potluck and how much she'd enjoyed the singing group. But after about five minutes her mien changed to a flat mask of glazed-eyed stillness.

Noticing that conversation had quieted in the seat behind me, I asked, "How are you doing, Tammy?" Only silence answered my question. Glancing in my rearview mirror, I saw Tammy's stiff posture gazing forward. I located Cindy in my mirror, and she shrugged her shoulders, looking back at me worriedly. Laura strained in her seat to see what was going on. Cindy leaned forward to whisper something to her.

"Tammy seems out of it, and Cindy's afraid she's going to have a seizure," Laura whispered to me.

At the next stoplight, I looked over my shoulder. Tammy was zombie-like; Cindy was frowning as she watched her. I asked, "Do you think we need to pull over somewhere?" I wasn't eager for a repeat performance of the morning.

"No, let's keep going. Nothing's happened yet," she answered. "I'll let you know if I think we should stop."

I continued down the street, glancing back and forth between the road and the mirror. The hushed atmosphere screamed with tension.

"She's asleep," Cindy said from the back. My mirror confirmed that Tammy's rigid posture was now slumped into the window, and her eyes were closed. Laura and I let out ragged breaths of gratitude for a slumbering Tammy rather than more seizures.

When we arrived at Tammy's building, waking her became a colossal task. She barely noticed our prodding and gentle shaking, as her head lolled to the side like an under-stuffed rag doll. After five minutes of nudging, she finally woke up enough to get out of the car. While Laura opened doors and pushed elevator buttons, Cindy and I braced Tammy up on either side as we maneuvered her unresponsive bulk into her apartment.

We plopped her down on the couch and looked around. Everything seemed just as we'd left it the night before when I'd picked Tammy up and took her to my house overnight. The birdcage was still covered with a white cloth, the dish rack was full of clean pans in the kitchen and the newspaper was still on the coffee table.

Tammy suddenly livened up and smiled at us as though she'd just noticed we were guests in her apartment. "Would you like a Popsicle?" she offered, getting up from the couch and moving towards her refrigerator.

We all looked at each other quizzically. *What is going on here? One minute she's like a zombie, the next she's asleep, and now she's the lively hostess.* "Tammy, we don't need Popsicles; we just finished eating. We came here to clean out your apartment, remember? You asked us to help you throw away your occult stuff," I gently reminded her.

"Oh yeah," she said, blinking.

"Tammy, you're going to have to help us. We don't know where everything is, and we don't exactly know what we're looking for," I prodded.

Tammy snapped to attention like a soldier obeying orders and moved towards the birdcage. "I have to uncover her first. Poor birdie, I bet you were lonely this morning," she crooned as she got some seed out to feed the silent bird on its perch.

Next she headed for the corner windows. "These owls have to go." She was all business as she reached up to unhook the hanging owls in the corner—three small cloth owls suspended inside a white cloth-covered hoop. "These are used in occult rituals; an owl's head can turn all the way around, you know." Her eyes flickered rather mockingly at me. "Rhonda, you had a nice owl hanging over my bed last night." I recoiled at the thought of my macramé owl hanging above the sofa bed at home.

"I'm sorry, Tammy. I had no idea. You should have told me; I would have taken it down." I made a mental note to do that when I got home, but right now something about Tammy was bothering me. Her helpful manner didn't mask the scorn I saw on her face.

"That's okay. I thought it was a pretty owl." Her sarcastic voice and taunting look seemed diametrically opposed to the task we came for. I stiffened in shock at this new Tammy that stood before me, and I wasn't quite sure how to continue. I was unprepared for her sudden changes and odd behavior.

Quickly, Tammy set the owls down on the coffee table and returned to the corner to grab a stuffed unicorn sprawled on the shelf under the windows. It was white with a golden horn and rainbow wings on it's sides. "This is also used by witches. Unicorns aren't real animals; they're magical, though. Rainbows are a symbol of the occult, too. " She stood stroking the unicorn's tail and its wings, then fingered the horn while she stared defiantly at me, mouth curled jeeringly.

The air in the room seemed as ominous and threatening as a dark thundercloud rolling in. We all stood rooted in our positions in the room. I could see Cindy and Laura out of the corners of my eyes, and they were as uncomfortable as I was. But I held Tammy's eyes, despite my confidence fraying around the edges. "I'll take the unicorn, Tammy," I said holding my hand out towards her.

She hesitated, sneer fading. Dropping the unicorn into my outstretched hand, she pivoted to face her bedroom. "I think I'll go lie down. I'm tired." She shuffled over to her bed and lay down facing the wall.

We all exchanged curious looks, not knowing what to do next.

"Squawk!" The sudden shriek came from the birdcage where the canary no longer sat huddled quietly on its perch. We all started at the sound and turned towards the cage. The bird was flailing back and forth, flying and banging against one side of the cage then the other, squawking with every hit.

Another sound came from Tammy's shaking bed where she lay vibrating. Startled by the suddenness of the onset of the seizures coupled with the noise from the cage, we just stood there transfixed for a moment. Cindy recovered first and said, "I'll go pray over her." She hurried to the bed, laid hands on Tammy and commanded any demonic activity to "Stop in the name of Jesus." Tammy immediately quieted and the pounding in the cage ceased simultaneously.

Tammy's seizures were becoming so ordinary to Cindy and I that we almost treated them as a matter of course. Cindy left Tammy resting on the bed while we continued with the search.

I found a brown paper grocery bag in the kitchen broom closet, stashed the owls and unicorn inside and placed it in front of the same doorless closet. We roamed the tiny apartment hunting for items that might be occult-oriented, but we really had no idea what we were looking for. Nothing seemed to leap out at us screaming, "Occult!"

"You can look in that walk-in closet," Tammy surprised us. She was up and heading for the kitchen. "Want a cupcake? They're left over from my birthday party Friday night." She stuck one in Laura's face, but Laura palmed it away from her.

"No, thank you, Tammy."

Unwrapping a cupcake for herself, Tammy said, "I put some of the stuff from Wicca in that closet."

I opened the closet door and walked in. Shelves lined the walls, and were filled mostly with canned goods, casserole dishes, pots and pans. But I did see a pile of papers that I lifted out and placed on the kitchen table to look through. Tammy hovered over me watching, munching and shifting her weight from one foot to the other. It seemed like the pile of Wicca lessons that Cindy had talked about.

"Those are my school papers," Tammy mumbled. I shuffled through astrological, numerology and palm reading charts and the many pages filled with writing and the Wicca name on top. Picking up the three-inch thick sheaf, I fit them into the waiting grocery bag.

Tammy watched me closely the whole time—her eyes and body following every move I made like my shadow. As I walked away from the closet, Tammy remained glued in front of it peering into the bag.

"What's wrong, Tammy?" I asked.

"That's my stuff in there," she said still stooped over the bag.

"Yes, it is."

"What are you going to do with it?"

"Remember, you asked us to come over and help you get rid of your occult objects? We're going to gather it together and throw it away for you." Tammy seemed like a child who continually needed to be reminded to pick up her toys.

Straightening up, she turned to me with opaque eyes. I couldn't tell if she understood what I'd just said or not. Her eyes seemed vaguely familiar, though. *Debbie and Cheryl. Her eyes look like theirs—vacant and empty.* I went over to her and placed my hand on her shoulder, "Are you okay, Tammy?"

"No." She stared at me with those vacant eyes.

"Would you like to sit down or lie down?"

Mechanically she trudged over to where Cindy sat on the couch reading her Bible. Not knowing exactly what would help Tammy at the moment, she read a few verses aloud starting from John 3:16. She kept reading to her until Tammy left her side.

We began to realize that the three of us each had a role to play that afternoon. Cindy's showed up first; she was the Bible and Prayer Lady. Throughout the afternoon, she searched her concordance for passages on witchcraft, demons, spiritual warfare—anything she thought we needed to hear at the time—and read them to us. She would spout verses to strengthen us when we became battle fatigued: "The Lord is my strength and my shield; my heart trusts in him, and I am helped," from Psalm 28:7. "All those gathered here will know that it is not by sword or spear that the Lord saves; for the battle is the Lord's," from 1 Samuel 17: 47. Cindy also shared the role with me of praying over Tammy when she had a seizure.

Tammy didn't remain by Cindy's side listening to the Bible for very long. She abruptly stood and went over to her bed.

"Squawk!" Bang! The canary's shrill complaint and frenzied flight drew our attention to Tammy's bed where she was stiffened in a seizure.

"My turn," I said, and went to pray over her. When Tammy stopped and became limp, the bird froze where it landed on the bottom of the cage.

The atmosphere was oppressive on Tammy's side of the apartment—her bedroom. I realized that we were in a war zone, and the battle line was drawn straight across the apartment between the living room and bedroom; there was a clear demarcation of whose side was whose. Tammy set up camp in her bedroom, which included the birdcage, and we stood our ground in the kitchen/living area. Her side of the apartment seemed like walking through a minefield into hand-to-hand combat with the war cries of the bird and the shaking bed for sound effects. Our territory was filled with the smoke and confusion of conflict; we were in the trenches. When Tammy crossed from her side to ours, she created skirmishes that were like small grass fires needing to be doused before they started the whole forest on fire. We each infiltrated the line at times, but retreating back into our own region of the apartment was always a relief.

I left Tammy resting in bed and disappeared into the walk-in closet. On hands and knees, I sifted through piles and boxes lined along the wall under the shelves. I searched through piles of bed linens, pillows, rags, clothing, and cartons of Christmas ornaments, knick-knacks, empty margarine tubs. After several minutes, I came out with the Ouija Board.

"Look what I found! It was hidden behind junk in the closet," I said holding up the prize to Cindy and Laura. I stuffed it in the grocery bag which was now becoming quite full.

Tammy was up again stirring around on her dresser top. She brought a small ivory-colored jewelry box over to the coffee table. "There's some jewelry in here I should get rid of." She opened it and drew out the necklace and matching ring with the tan-veined stones that Cindy had seen two weeks ago and handed them to Laura. Next she brought out a crystal pendant necklace and relinquished that one to my open palm. "If you rub that, it can do all sorts of things for you."

"Like what, Tammy?" I said.

"It can bring you good luck. It's supposed to be full of energy, so when you rub it, the crystal gives off energy for your body and mind. I guess it has healing powers, but it never worked for me."

She found a couple of other pieces of jewelry in her box that seemed very normal to all of us. We never would have guessed that they were used somehow in occult or witchcraft practices. Tammy gave vague explanations of what they were used for, saying, "Maybe good luck, or maybe in rituals; I don't really remember."

All the jewelry ended up in the grocery bag.

Tammy stood and looked longingly beyond us at her bed as though something were calling her towards it. "I'm tired." She plodded over to it and lay down.

We nervously looked at each other until the scream of the bird made us jump. Wham! Against the sides of the cage in harsh protests, the bird crashed its little body back and forth.

"I believe it's my turn," Cindy said. She went into the enemy camp to stop the combat. And the silenced canary huddled in a corner of the cage.

Shrugging off the tension like a heavy coat, I went back into the closet to see what else I could find. Fifteen minutes later, I came up empty. "I can't find anything else in there," I said. "I've moved stuff around and looked behind things, but no luck."

Laura searched the bookshelf and then the kitchen cupboards, but she also found nothing.

"I wonder where those candles are. They have to be in this apartment somewhere." Cindy was on her hands and knees searching under the furniture. When she was between the couch and coffee table, peering under the couch, Tammy silently crept up behind her and bent over her.

"What are you looking for?" Tammy's voice was so close to her ear that it startled Cindy causing her to jerk and hit her head on the coffee table.

"Ow! Tammy, don't scare me like that," Cindy said rubbing her head.

"Did I scare you?" Tammy asked with a smirk on her face.

"Tammy," I said, steering her away from Cindy, "We're still trying to find some of your occult objects, but we can't seem to find anything else."

"And you think there's stuff under the couch?" she huffed. "You guys are dumb."

"Okay, why don't you show us where things are? Then we can help you get rid of it all." I tried to soothe the angry look in her eyes.

Tammy crossed the line into her bedroom. But this time she didn't go to the bed; instead, she just stood there gazing around her. She had a faraway look in her eyes, and she stopped and cocked her head. Her eyes riveted to the corner window.

The three of us watched her to see what would happen next. Quickly, Tammy glided over to the window, grabbed the white ceramic dove that sat on the shelf, pivoted on her heel and headed to the kitchen. Opening the refrigerator, she placed the dove on a shelf and slammed the door shut. Wiping and clapping her hands together, she said, "There!"

I went over to her and gently put my hand on her shoulder, but she didn't meet my gaze. "Tammy, why did you put the dove in the refrigerator?"

"I needed to cool that dove down. He was getting way too hot!" she said smiling through me with her flat eyes. She was in a dark zone that we couldn't enter—nor did we want to.

What an odd thing to say! I'm not about to let her keep that dove in the fridge. With one hand around Tammy's shoulders, I opened the refrigerator door and took out the dove and held it in my other hand before her. "I like this dove, Tammy. Do you know that the dove is a symbol for the Holy Spirit? Didn't you tell me that your grandmother bought you this dove?"

Trying to snatch the dove out of my hand, she parroted, "That dove's too hot. We really need to cool it down."

I held tightly to the dove and managed to place it on the kitchen counter behind me and physically turn Tammy away from it. Tammy began wandering around the apartment while we observed her every move.

The three of us stared uncomfortably at each other, shrugging shoulders and shaking heads. The dove incident was like something out of the *Twilight Zone.* The afternoon was twisting into an eerie nightmare. We began to feel as though we were dodging sniper bullets; everything godly was under attack—including us.

Tammy began fighting her own battle, and it appeared that we were losing ground with her. She was in her own little world, listening to familiar voices and heeding unheard words. As she roamed the perimeter of the apartment touching everything she passed, her footsteps took on their normal heaviness. Soon she headed for the bed and began another attack. And the bird went nuts.

I sighed. "I'll take care of her." Tammy had so many seizures that afternoon that we lost count. With familiarity, she went to her bed, lay down, began a seizure, the bird screamed and bounced around in the cage, then froze when Tammy stopped after we prayed over her.

Besides praying over Tammy and gathering occult items in the grocery bag, I seemed to have the role of Spokes Lady. After the bizarre incident with the dove, Cindy called me Velvet Mouth. Somehow throughout the afternoon, it was my job to handle Tammy verbally. I always had the right words to calm her, the perfect questions to ask her and Tammy listened to me. I knew, though, that the words were God-chosen and flowed from my mouth only by His direction, and I was calm and self-assured in the role.

Cindy was furiously looking up passages in her Bible, reading off encouraging words to us when she found something. "Psalm 18 is a good one. 'I love you, O Lord, my strength. The Lord is my rock, my fortress and my deliverer; my God is my rock, in whom I take refuge. He is my shield and the horn of my salvation, my stronghold.'" She continued reading all fifty verses while we allowed it to wash over and into us like sunshine parting the thick clouds. We needed to hear Scripture at that moment and wanted the Word to permeate the room—including Tammy's side of the apartment.

Suddenly Tammy whipped past us in the living room and disappeared into the walk-in closet. We heard rummaging in there, so I went over to see what she was doing. She nearly knocked me down as she blasted out of there with both hands full of candles.

Black taper candles. Red taper candles. Red witch-shaped candle. And the dreaded gold skull. She dumped them on the kitchen table with a triumphant gloat. She seemed proud of her cache like a pirate who'd just found the hidden treasure.

My mouth gaped open at the colorful array before me. *Where had those candles come from? I searched that closet.* I collected my wits and asked, "Where were these candles in the closet, Tammy?"

"On the top shelf."

"But I looked in there and didn't find them."

She twisted her mouth into an ugly smile. "They were behind a few things." She began placing the black taper candles into the base that the skull rested on. Then she drew away from the table and whisked over to the kitchen cupboards and began opening and slamming drawers and doors.

"What are you looking for, Tammy?" I asked.

"I need some matches. I'm going to light up the candles."

"That's not a good idea. Why don't you see if there's anything else in the closet that I missed?"

"No. I need some matches. I'm going to light that skull up."

"Tammy," I said, gently guiding her away from the cupboards, "Let's search the closet together. We don't need to light any candles right now."

She allowed me to turn her away from the kitchen, but she apprehended the skull as we went by the table. "I need to warm him up," she said as she palmed the skull and began petting it.

"Tammy, give me the skull."

She ignored me and hugged it tightly to her chest.

I reconnoitered and tried to advance from a different angle. "Can I look at the skull, Tammy? Cindy told me about it, but I haven't had a good look at it."

She coyly looked at me under her lashes as if she weren't sure she believed me. I held out my open palm. She slowly relinquished it as though it were her favorite toy.

"I don't feel well." She traipsed over and sank onto her bed. My nerves were already coming unhinged, and the shrieking bird didn't help. It commenced its frenzied banging while Tammy began to shake. I sighed and looked over my shoulder at Cindy.

She got up from the couch and laid hands on Tammy, commanding whatever evil force lurked there to "Stop!" Tammy stopped. The canary came to rest on its perch.

I went over to the cage and peered at the tiny yellow fluff of feathers. "What is wrong with this bird?"

Cindy and Laura gathered beside me. "I don't know," Cindy said tiredly. "It's as though it's connected to Tammy somehow. Every time she has a seizure, it goes crazy."

"Do you suppose there's some kind of curse on it?" Laura offered.

"Of course! Tammy's two witch friends gave it to her. They must have done something to the bird—cursed it or said some kind of incantation over it," I said. "We need help. I don't know what to do anymore. Tammy's getting weirder by the minute."

"Remember Mary?" Cindy asked. Laura and I nodded; Mary had belonged to our church and we'd all been in Evangelism Explosion together. "What if we called her?" Cindy laughed nervously, "She's charismatic; she might know something."

"I'll look up her number," Laura moved to the phone in the corner where she threw open the phone book and flipped the pages, searching. Although Laura helped me with the gathering of the occult paraphernalia, her main role became the Phone Lady.

"Found it," she said after a few moments.

We were all desperate for some kind of help—any kind of help. We felt as though we were drowning in the trenches.

Mary was home, and Laura tried to explain what was going on with Tammy. While she was on the phone and Cindy hovered close to hear what she had to say, I paced the room.

I was uneasy to the point of exploding. Or tears. Neither would help. I spotted the candles. *They have to be destroyed.* God was nudging my energy towards demolishing the candles. I snapped every taper candle in two and dropped the pieces into the grocery bag. There was no way to break the skull—it was probably four inches wide—so I simply buried it in the bag. I moved the witch candle over to the cutting board beside the sink. It was a wax figurine about seven inches tall and perhaps two inches thick. Finding a knife in one of the drawers, I drew it out.

"What are you doing?" Cindy asked.

"I think I have to cut the head off this candle," I said.

"Why?"

"It needs to be destroyed."

Cindy nodded. "That makes sense." And I cut off the head and added the pieces to the bag. My mind ran wild with the idea of Tammy using the knife as a weapon, and it sent prickles of fear trickling up my spine. I cleaned off the knife and put it back in the drawer.

Laura said, "Mary says Tammy needs deliverance."

"What's that?" Cindy and I asked simultaneously.

"Tammy could be possessed and need demons cast out."

"We've done that, haven't we?" Cindy and I asked each other.

And Tammy had another seizure—this time we both went over and began casting out demons with renewed fervor. Tammy stopped her spasm, but we continued praying over her. We commanded. We prayed. We were exhausted, so we let Tammy sleep then collapsed on the couch.

"Mary says we need to pray the blood of Jesus over ourselves for protection against the demons." Laura began relaying the verses that Mary gave her, and Cindy wrote them down on a pad of paper she drew from her Bible cover. "Romans 3:25 and 5:9; Ephesians 2:13; Hebrews 9—just read the whole thing; Revelation 1:5, 5:9, 7:14, 12:10-12."

Even though the concept was totally new to us, Cindy and I jumped on praying the blood of Jesus over the three of us. We'd never heard of doing that before, but we were at an impasse and willing to try anything. Laura continued on the phone for a while longer before hanging up, but Tammy was up and roving again. A cryptic smile perched on her lips. She stopped in front of the birdcage, face up against the wires and whispered to the bird. "I think I'm going to change her name," she said to us. "Her new name is Demona."

Demona. Sounds too close to demon for my liking. "That doesn't sound like a good name to me, Tammy. Can't you think of a better name to call it?"

"Demona," Tammy breathed out emphatically. "I like Demona; it fits." She waggled her finger at the bird. "Hi, Demona. You like your new name, don't you?"

Nonchalantly, Tammy sidled past the wall next to the broom closet, reached up with her right hand while looking straight ahead, slipped the Christian calendar off the nail on the wall and hid the calendar between the refrigerator and the broom closet without missing a step. Next stop was the wall behind the dining room table where she surreptitiously slid the Christian plaque off its nail and casually moved over to the couch and dropped it behind the couch.

Cindy and I were watching this new display with trepidation. We both realized what Tammy was doing. She was like a sniper finding her targets—anything Christian—and zinging each one. She walked past the couch, picked up the newspaper that was lying on the end of it, doubled back, opened the newspaper and arranged it calmly over Cindy's open Bible.

This made Cindy angry; she wasn't about to let Tammy cover up the Word of God. She determinedly folded the newspaper and placed it on the coffee table. Tammy noticed and tried again.

Taking the paper, she spread it open and patted it firmly down over the Bible.

"Oh, Tammy, you get the newspaper," Cindy said as she persistently lifted it up and pretended to read it. Tammy's eyes were fixed bayonets aimed at the Bible. Cindy then tucked the paper under her leg, picked up her Bible and placed it on her lap and smiled up at Tammy who headed for her bed.

Demona screamed a strangled discord and bashed herself back and forth against the cage. Tammy's seizures seemed to be getting more violent, thrashing and heaving her body against the wall beside the bed. But God was faithful, and every time we prayed over her, the seizures stopped.

While Cindy took care of Tammy, I replaced the Christian calendar and plaque. Then the three of us stood in the center of the living room and prayed. "What are we going to do?" Laura asked.

"We can't leave her like this," I said.

"On Tammy's bulletin board is a card that says *Love Lines*; I noticed it when I was on the phone with Mary earlier. Maybe we should try that number and see if they have any suggestions," Laura said.

None of us knew anything about *Love Lines*, but we were grasping at anything we thought might help. So Laura got on the phone again. She explained that we were with a young woman who'd been in the occult and was manifesting seizures every fifteen to twenty minutes. Laura didn't have to go any further. "She needs deliverance," said the lady on the phone. "Here's a number of a church you can call to get help. They might not be there this afternoon, but I'm sure someone will be there tonight."

Laura relayed the message to us. That was the second time we'd heard the word *deliverance* that day. Maybe there was more to this deliverance business than we were aware of. Laura tried calling the number, but there was no answer.

Tammy was up. The Christian calendar casually came down. Tammy went by the refrigerator and grabbed a grape Popsicle from the freezer, unwrapped it and stuck it in her mouth. The Christian plaque dropped behind the couch again, and the newspaper that Cindy previously sat on now covered the Bible again as Tammy strolled the room.

"I made a blood oath to Satan, you know," Tammy threw at us.

"No, Tammy, we didn't know that. When did you do that?" I asked with more serenity than I felt. This latest tidbit seemed like the last block added to a tower before it toppled.

Tapping the Popsicle against her lip, she paused as though deciding whether to say more or not. "When I was with Jan at her meeting once. She pricked my finger and collected my blood in a little dish, then I wrote out my name in my own blood in a big book they had."

"What kind of book was it, Tammy?"

"They called it Satan's book. My name's in the book. Forever." She gazed into another dimension with glossed eyes.

I was raveling around the edges. *We need help. We need it now.* I glanced at Laura. She mouthed, "Still no answer."

"Tammy, remember when I first met you?" She nodded. "We prayed together that night, and you turned your life over to Jesus, remember?"

Tammy stiffened, "I'm tired." She headed to her stronghold, and the attack took hold. I thought the canary would die soon if it had to go through more bashing. While I prayed over Tammy, Cindy read the Bible verses given to us out loud. Laura decided to call *Love Lines* again. "There's no answer at that church. Is there anyone else who can help us?" They gave her the number of an Assemblies of God church nearby.

While she was dialing, I felt a distinct, strong urge to get up and stand in front of the sack of trash where we were collecting Tammy's occult paraphernalia. I obeyed the urge without question, and took my place in front of the bag as sentinel on guard duty.

"What are you doing?" Cindy asked.

"Well, I don't know exactly," I replied a bit sheepishly. "But I think God wants me to stand in front of this bag." I held up my invisible shield in front of my body with my left hand and wielded my invisible sword with my right hand.

Cindy whipped through pages in her Bible and stopped at Ephesians 6. "Finally, be strong in the Lord and in his mighty power. Put on the full armor of God so that you can take your stand against the devil's schemes." And she continued reading the rest of the chapter aloud.

"That's what I'm doing," I said. "Standing with my armor on."

Meanwhile, Laura had reached someone at the church and was relaying our problem.

The reason for my guard duty soon became apparent as Tammy churned around the corner. She paced in front of me like a lion ready to pounce. "I want my Ouija Board," she said pointing over my shoulder.

Fully girded, I was unruffled by her demand. "No, Tammy, you can't have it." As I watched Tammy mark out a semicircle around me, but two feet away from me, I realized that she could deck me if she wanted to. She was larger than I, and I wasn't about to slug it out with her.

"I want my Ouija Board," she said with more emphasis, jabbing her finger as though she were trying to poke through the unseen protective shield in front of me. Even her finger couldn't penetrate the buffer zone that God had placed around me.

"No," I said. I couldn't believe how peaceful I was inside. *She can't get to me. God is not going to let her touch me.*

It was as though we were playing a game where I was queen of the mountain, but Tammy wasn't allowed to come within two feet of me. As Tammy walked from one side to the other, I would step slightly so that I always faced her. Peering and pointing around me at the sack of trash, she feigned calm, but her voice rose to a new level as she spewed out through gritted teeth, "I *want* my Ouija Board."

"No, Tammy. I won't give you your Ouija Board."

God enveloped me as powerfully as His cloud shielded the Israelites from the Egyptians. Tammy could not puncture the strong hedge of protection surrounding me. I almost cried at the sheer weight and glory of His presence. He was so real! I was awed by how much He cared about *me* standing in front of that bag of occult stuff. God's mighty power to fend off all the evil reigning in the room amazed me. I watched Tammy circle one more time before giving up. I stood. Against evil powers, I stood my ground. And it changed my life. My God was bigger and more powerful than I ever gave Him credit for. He had been there for me when I needed Him most. And by His authority, I stood firm.

"They're coming. I reached a pastor and he's coming with a team," Laura announced, hanging up the phone.

Cindy and I exhaled loudly. Clenching her fists by her side, Tammy wheeled on Laura, "Who's coming? I don't want anybody else to come to my apartment. I didn't invite anyone." She turned to me, "Tell her to call them back. I won't let anyone in. You had no right!"

"Tammy, it'll be all right," I said trying to ease her anger which threatened to explode like a grenade. "They'll be friendly people. You'll like them. Besides, I'm sure they've already left. If you don't like them when they get here, I'll send them home, okay?"

I appeased her for the moment. She stood nose to her birdcage and whispered to Demona who didn't even twitter. Then she moved to her bed and stiffened and shook in a seizure, and Demona shrieked. Cindy tended Tammy this time. I remained rooted in position in front of the grocery bag.

We decided that we were done collecting occult items. Without Tammy's help, we had no hope of finding more to get rid of. We waited and prayed. The battle was taking its toll on the three of us, and we eagerly awaited our relief troops. Tammy remained still in her bed.

Rap, rap, rap. *Finally, help is here.* Cindy opened the door for three people—a young male pastor and another man and a woman. They introduced themselves to us as they squeezed into Tammy's tiny kitchen. Because the space was so small, in order to let them all into the apartment, I left my sentry duty in front of the bag in the closet and moved into the living room. Tammy flashed around the corner, grabbed her Ouija Board, ran back to her bed and curled up in a fetal position facing the wall, hugging her Ouija Board to her chest before I even had time to think. I'd never seen this slow-moving girl act so quickly before.

We explained the situation to the threesome. The pastor, Steve, informed us that witches put a type of "blessing" on a pet—causing it to be possessed by a demon—and it becomes what is called a "familiar." The pet then is psychically sensitive to and acts in accordance with its owner.[2] That's why the bird was raucous when Tammy was in the throes of a seizure; it was doing what Tammy was doing. Sometimes these pets are used as an aid to witches in their rites. He said we should get the bird out of the apartment because of the familiar demons attached to both the bird and Tammy. He also said that we should try to get the Ouija Board back.

But first we gathered in a circle while our visitors prayed for us, for Tammy, for the situation. Bolstered a bit, I went over to Tammy's bed with Steve. "Tammy," he said, "Will you give us the Ouija Board?"

No answer.

"Tammy, we're here to help you. We want to pray for you and help you get rid of the demons that are bothering you and making you seizure."

Tammy lay tightly curled and didn't respond.

"Tammy, Jesus wants you free from demons."

Bam! She shook violently, hugging the Ouija Board in a death grip. Steve stood and watched her, listening to Demona screeching and watching her flail against the sides of the cage. "Get that bird out of here," he said. Laura and the woman complied, picking up the cage and stepping outside the apartment door. I then explained how we coped with Tammy's seizures. I commanded the demons to stop in Jesus' name. And they did.

He tried wrenching the Ouija Board out of her hands, since she appeared limp. But Tammy fought and held on tightly, turning again toward the wall.

We held a conference in the living room. Steve decided that we should gather Tammy's occult paraphernalia and throw it away in the dumpster right then. I picked it up, and we were on our way towards the elevator with the bag and the bird, when Tammy came screaming down the hallway. "Give me back my bird!"

She was riled up and spitting expletives. A few doors opened up along the hallway, and inquisitive faces poked out. She caused such a scene that Steve decided to bring it all back into her apartment. We marched back down the hall and into Tammy's apartment. It felt like defeat. Laura placed the cage back where she got it. I tried to calm Tammy who ignored me. The room was a chaotic bedlam of people and explosive words. The conflict was escalating out of control and I was nearing the panic level and about ready to wave the white flag.

"Get out!" She ranted and strode from one side of the room to the other, still clutching her Ouija Board. Then she turned on me.

"You said you'd tell them to leave if I didn't like them. Get them out of here!" she yelled.

She returned to her fetal position on her bed and while she had the seizure, Steve forced the Ouija Board out of her hands and put it back into the grocery bag. Cindy took care of her, with the other guy looking on and praying.

We convened again in the middle of the living room. Things were intensifying, careening out of control like a large rock rolling downhill and picking up speed. Yet we weren't making any progress with Tammy.

Tammy whipped around the corner again and lifted her Ouija Board out of the bag. Steve made a grab for it. Tammy yelled at him. Still clenching it in her crossed arms, she hurried to her bed and returned to her familiar fetal position. We all stared at each other. What now?

Evil hung in the air like thick cobwebs waiting to entrap us. I rubbed my arms as I shivered. The small grass fires had turned into a blazing bonfire, and we could almost smell the acrid stench. Running my hands through my hair, I announced, "I'm going to try one more time."

Standing over Tammy's hunched form I cajoled, "Tammy, please let us help you." She rocked back and forth. "Tammy, these demons are harassing you. Don't you want to be set free?"

Then she spoke in a voice that lives in my nightmares, that spiraled eerily out of her mouth and dissipated like a puff of smoke, that raised an octave and chanted lazily, saying, "I *am* free."

I'll never forget that wafting, slithering voice that crawled into the center of my memory and lodged there. I half expected to see the ugly black demons that were torturing Tammy to vomit out of her mouth and fly around the room. I was done. I was spooked and decided on a full retreat. The battle seemed over. We'd done all we could do, and it was time to go.

And I pivoted and faced the group. "I'm leaving."

I grabbed my jacket off the back of a kitchen chair, picked up the bag of occult stuff and walked out the door. In a bevy of activity behind me, everyone followed.

"I can't leave that Ouija Board in there," Steve declared. And he went back in and forced it out of her unsuspecting arms. She was up in a shot, white-hot daggers shooting from her eyes and ghastly speech spraying from her mouth.

Steve backed towards the open door to the apartment. Tammy smacked him with her open hand, knocking his glasses sideways, breaking them and leaving a thin streak of blood trickling down the side of his face. He spilled into us in the hallway and slammed the door shut just as Tammy threw a pan that struck it with a clatter.

The battle had turned ugly and bloody. Steve took out his handkerchief and wiped his face. His glasses would need major repair. We collectively let out frazzled breaths. I felt like collapsing right there in the hallway outside Tammy's door.

Then from within the apartment we heard deep, wrenching sobs. Then wailing that tore at my heart. "What's that about?" I asked Steve.

"There's a tug-of-war going on within Tammy. That's what you experienced in there today. She gave her life to Jesus when you prayed for her that first day, but the old demons still have a hold on her. She gave her life to Satan first and he isn't about to give up on her. He has a right to her. It's hard for her to leave what's familiar, and today Satan won. But she's sobbing because there's still a part of her that wants Jesus."

We listened for a while outside her door. Then the sobbing was replaced with another sound. *Tap, tap. Tap, tap. Tap, tap.* The rhythmic noise came from just inside the door, like a plastic cup rapping on her kitchen table.

"Okay, that's probably table tapping," Steve said. "Let's go."

We dropped off the sack of stuff—owls, unicorn, papers, jewelry, candles, Ouija Board—in the dumpster outside the building; only the bird remained in Tammy's apartment. Then we stood around in the parking lot talking. Steve left us with this advice: "Read your Bibles. Read everything you can find about the Holy Spirit."

Laura, Cindy and I climbed dejectedly into my blue van for the quiet ride home. We were each caught up in our own thoughts. We didn't know what to say to each other, how to make sense of the situation, so we didn't try.

We lingered in the empty church parking lot as I dropped Laura off to finish some work at school. We didn't want to say goodbye. Somehow we were safer in each other's company. But Laura went into the building, and I took Cindy home. She lived only a half mile from me. I tarried in her driveway, wanting to fill the empty spot in the pit of my stomach. We talked a little while, but then she went into her house and I drove home.

I slumped into the steering wheel. *What a depressing day.* It was almost 6:30. We'd been at Tammy's for 5 hours. The last two weeks and especially that afternoon seemed like wasted time with Tammy. As far as I knew, she'd made her choice, and it was Satan, not Jesus. I wasn't sure I ever wanted to see her again.

The people I desired to see were my husband and children. I needed hugs—and food—I was starving. The activity of the afternoon had burned up my lunch calories and then some. As I entered my house, I expected relief from my gloomy mood, but a heavy, stifling feeling overcame me. Fear was lurking behind my front door, waiting to clutch and claw at my already raw nerves like a monster on the attack. The day wasn't over yet.

[2] Lewis, James R.<u>Witchcraft Today: An Encyclopedia of Wiccan and Neopagan Traditions</u>. Santa Barbara: ABC-CLIO, 1999.

Chapter Six

FEAR AND CLEANSING

...but we were harassed at every turn—conflicts on the outside, fears within.
2 Corinthians 7:5b

There is no fear in love. But perfect love drives out fear, because fear has to do with punishment. The one who fears is not made perfect in love.
1 John 4:18

Closing the front door of my house, I stared gloomily down the seven steps to the lower level, shivered and hugged myself as I rubbed my arms. Tammy had slept down there. I couldn't see the hide-a-bed around the corner, but the thought of it brought back the picture of Tammy having seizures and foaming at the mouth. It seemed like a dark, dank, dirty dungeon now with unknown monsters hiding in corners, even though it was walkout level with plenty of windows. *I'll deal with the bed later. I can't go down there right now.*

"Mommy!" squealed my four-year-old Rachel at the top of the stairs. She flung out her arms, little fingers pinching air like a lobster's claw opening and closing.

Her cherubic voice ended my reverie. I smiled and tromped up the steps with my own arms outstretched. "Rachel!" I said trying to match her zeal. I lifted her off her feet and swung her around as she giggled with glee. It felt good to be hugged by innocence. The scene and atmosphere in my own living room was a stark contrast to Tammy's apartment. The only battleground here was picking my way through toys cluttering the room. Derek was sprawled on the floor erecting some kind of Lego construction in the middle of the room, Dawn had commandeered a corner of the couch for her dolls and their clothes and Rachel must have been "reading" through her pile of books. The mess was as beautiful to me as a garden full of bright flowers.

I put Rachel down and gave my other two children squeezes before falling into my husband's arms and hanging on. His strong arms gave strength to my flagging body and spirit. I needed someone stronger than me right now.

"We waited for you, but the kids got hungry so I made a pizza. We just finished eating, but there's still some left if you're hungry," Darrell said into my hair as he rubbed my back.

"I'm starving," I said pulling away and brushing away a lone tear that had glided down my cheek like drizzled icing.

The kids went back to playing while Darrell and I went into the kitchen. "What happened?" he asked. "I didn't expect you to be gone so long."

"I didn't either," I said as I took the pizza out of the fridge, popped it into the microwave and punched buttons.

We sat down at the table, and I began retelling the events of the afternoon as best I could in between bites of pepperoni pizza. I was ravenous as I downed three pieces and a can of pop. The events of the afternoon all tumbled out of my mouth like Derek's Legos strewn about the floor. The bird, Tammy's attitude, the occult stuff being collected in the grocery bag, Tammy's seizures, our helpers and the violent end. I tried to take all the right pieces and fit them together in the correct order to reconstruct the story so that it made sense.

"So what do you do now?" he asked.

"The pastor said we should read everything we can about the Holy Spirit and the occult from the Bible and Christian books."

"But what about Tammy? What do you do about her? Are you going to call her again?"

"*I'm* not going to call her. She made her choice today, and it wasn't Jesus. I don't think I want to see her again," I said pushing my chair away from the table for emphasis.

Darrell let it go at that and went back into the living room.

I did busywork in the kitchen awhile, putting away my dishes, wiping the table, cleaning up a bit until I ran out of things to do. Then I went into the bathroom and looked at the strain of the day reflecting back at me from the mirror. Dark brows squinting together over my bloodshot eyes, down-turned mouth unable to capture enough energy to keep a smile. I felt dirty—like an unseen black dust had settled into every pore. There was something on me that needed to be scrubbed off, so I washed my face, holding the warm cloth over it, letting the heat sink in. I still felt polluted. I repeated the process, but I couldn't cleanse Tammy or the day off me.

I went into the living room and sat down on the couch next to Darrell, hoping his proximity would help me feel normal again. I crossed my legs and rhythmically swung the one on top. I picked at my nails. I ran my hands through my dark hair. I thought of the hide-a-bed in the basement. The specter of Tammy having a seizure entered the room and displayed itself before me. *I need to wash those sheets. And the blanket. And the pillow. And she wore my sweater.*

"You seem awfully antsy," Darrell said.

I stopped biting my nails. "Did you put the hide-a-bed up? I need to wash the sheets that were on it."

"No, I didn't get around to doing it. I thought you'd want to wash things."

"I think I need to wash everything she touched—the pillow, blanket, my sweater."

"I don't think you need to go that far, Rhonda."

I stood and tread a path into the rust and brown carpet in front of the couch. "Yeah, I do. Everything needs to be washed. Everything feels soiled. I feel dirty, like a leper in the Bible. I should go around shouting, 'Unclean, unclean,' so everybody stays away from me. My whole house feels unclean," I said, flinging my arms to encompass the space. "Maybe if I wash it all, then I'll feel better."

"Aren't you going a bit overboard?" Darrell asked, rising from the couch with a concerned look on his face.

"You weren't there today. You didn't see what I saw or feel what I felt. I just need to feel clean again. I have to do something," I said raising my voice a level. Tears threatened to spill out. I thought of losing it and crumpling to the floor in a heap, but I held on to the thread that my emotions were dangling from because the kids were in the room. They'd all three stopped playing to look at me.

"Is Mommy okay?" Rachel asked, looking as though she was about to cry.

"Mommy's all right. She's just a little upset; go back to reading your book," Darrell answered her. Turning to me and putting his arm around me, he said, "All right. Do whatever makes you feel better. Do you need my help?"

"No, I can do it. The sweater's in the bedroom." I turned down the hall and retrieved the ivory sweater that I'd crocheted myself. Then I hovered on the edge of the top step, clutching the wrought iron railing. "Okay, I'm going downstairs now," I said staring down the staircase as though I were on a cliff looking into a shadowy abyss and afraid of falling in.

Darrell just looked at me quizzically as I headed down the stairs slowly. *I don't know why I needed to tell him I was going downstairs. He knows I'm going down here. What am I so afraid of?*

At the bottom step, I hesitated. An eerie sensation snaked its way under my skin and wrapped itself around my psyche. I cringed at the perturbing pictures that swirled in my imagination—Tammy's strange demeanor, her bird crashing around in its cage, Tammy having a seizure. Trying to wipe out the images like spots on a mirror, I closed my eyes tightly and prayed a Lord-help-me prayer in gulping breaths. Gradually the fears receded back into the gloom they'd come from, and I was able to inhale and exhale rhythmically again.

I unclenched my hold on the railing and stepped into the family room and inspected the offending bed and linens. Anger at Tammy crept into action, and I attacked the bed linens, wrenching them off the bed in one large wadded-up lump. Crossing over to the laundry room, I started the water, poured in detergent, then stuffed sheets and blanket, pillow and sweater all into the large machine. I ceremonially smacked my hands together as though rubbing off grime into the washer, then banged the lid shut.

Turning again towards the bed, I lifted the end, folding it onto itself then grabbed the handhold and quickly shoved the bed down into the couch. I hurried to push the cushions back into place over the bed, half expecting to see black things crawling out from underneath it and picking their way into the room. *No creeping, slithering beings here.* I felt like the kid who'd just conquered the monsters under her bed. The room looked normal again, and I felt more at ease with the idea of my children sleeping in their rooms down the hall.

It was bedtime for the girls, so I went upstairs to help them clean up their toys. The phone rang; it was Laura. While I talked to her, Darrell readied the girls for bed.

Laura had gone into her classroom to do some work after I dropped her off at church; her husband was out of town, and she wasn't ready to face an empty house alone. But she couldn't stop thinking about Tammy. She'd been fighting fears just as I had. Interrupting her preparations for the next school day, she prayed asking God for help in clearing her mind and erasing her fears. God reminded her of one of her kindergarten student's father, a youth pastor at a nearby church. She remembered from talking with him that he'd dealt with the occult in his work with some kids in his youth group. Taking the chance that he'd be home, she decided to call him and tell him about our experience with Tammy that afternoon.

"Rhonda, he thinks we all ought to gather at your house tonight and pray; he's willing to come over to talk and pray with us."

"I don't know. It's getting late. I'm exhausted; aren't you tired?"

"Well, let me put it this way—will you be able to sleep tonight?"

Fear was already rooting inside of me, sending down a tentacle like a dandelion clinging to the rich, dark soil of my imagination. Even though I'd pulled up the weed, the root had already dug deep and was sending up new shoots despite my washing all that Tammy had touched. "Okay, if you think it'll help us. I'm awfully jittery—and scared. Why my house, anyway? Shouldn't we meet at church?"

"He said we should meet at your house because Tammy stayed there. He wants to pray over your house and van. I'll call Cindy, then call Ray back. We should be over there in about half an hour, all right?"

"Okay. Maybe this will help me." As I hung up, I felt a deep sense of relief to have someone who knew what he was doing come over and pray over my house—and me. Maybe I wasn't going overboard with feeling dirty after all.

I lingered over the girls' bedtime story that night, savoring their purity and clean-smelling little bodies. Their childish prayers were like a lullaby to my overly stimulated ears. After closing their bedroom door, I walked to the laundry room and opened the washer, taking out the linens and throwing them in the dryer. I figured the hot dryer would kill any lingering, demon germs. Derek was out of the shower and ready for bed also, so I kissed him good night, tucked him in and prayed with him. "You have a half hour to read, then you need to turn out the light," I said before closing his door.

I barely had time to sit down upstairs when the doorbell rang. Darrell let in Cindy, Laura and Ray, a broad bear of a man. Laura introduced us all to Ray, explaining that she'd called him to ask him some questions about Tammy's involvement in the occult.

"After Laura explained what went on at Tammy's," Ray said, "I knew that you ladies needed cleansing from any demons that might have attached themselves to you. I asked Laura if the other pastor had prayed over you, and she said he hadn't. So I asked if she'd mind if I did it for you."

Darrell had his wits about him and remembered his manners, inviting them all to sit down in the living room. I was still on edge and listened attentively to Ray's forthright, knowledgeable voice. "What do you mean *cleansing?*" I asked before Ray even sat down.

"How much do you all know about dealing with someone who's been involved in the occult?" he asked.

"A little more than we did two weeks ago," I piped in dryly. We all laughed nervously.

Cindy offered, "We were told that Tammy needed deliverance because she was probably possessed. We know that when we command the demons to stop, Tammy's seizures will stop. We believe her seizures are not medical—the doctors told her that anyway—but that they're demonic in nature."

"I told Ray all about what went on at Tammy's apartment today, and how it ended," Laura added to Cindy and I.

Then Ray leaned forward with his forearms on his knees and began teaching us about what we'd gotten ourselves into. "First of all, let me say that I admire you ladies for getting involved with Tammy—a lot of people might have been scared off by her background. Now that you're in pretty deep, I think there's some things you ought to understand.

"It does sound as though Tammy could be possessed—at the very least she's being oppressed and harassed by demons. This is happening to Tammy because of her involvement in the occult. She gave her life to Satan and he has rights to her now and apparently isn't giving her up without a fight. I want you to know that it's good that you got help today, and it's okay that you left Tammy's when you did. You touched the garment of Satan this afternoon, and it sounds like you did all you could today."

Cindy, Laura, Darrell and I leaned in to grasp hold of everything Ray had to say. His assurances of what we'd done with Tammy so far were like bandages to our open wounds and glue to our frayed nerves.

"I'd like to pray for each of you to be baptized with the Holy Spirit," he said. "The Holy Spirit will come over you with power and help you as you minister with Tammy. Have you ever heard of the baptism with the Holy Spirit? Would you like me to pray for you to receive it?"

We looked back and forth at each other. Cindy said, "I've heard of it before—from Mary." She looked over at me, and I nodded. I'd heard Mary mention it also, but I had never quite comprehended all of what she was talking about. Cindy continued, almost thinking out loud, "There was a group of people Bruce and I knew in college; they were charismatic and talked about the Holy Spirit all the time. They were a little strange." She looked quizzically at Ray.

"They might have been baptized in the Spirit. Sometimes people find them a little unconventional," he said.

Cindy looked down at her loafers while everyone waited for her answer. "It's not that I don't want to receive it; it's just that I promised my husband before I left that I wouldn't do anything like that without him. He's a little freaked out by what's going on." She hesitated again. "So I guess I'm going to say no tonight," she said in a quiet voice.

Ray looked at Laura who shook her head no. "I don't think so—not right now, anyway."

"Okay, we won't pray for that then," he said.

"Hold it," I spoke up. "You didn't ask me!" I was a bit indignant to be overlooked like that. Maybe I didn't understand all of what the baptism with the Holy Spirit was, but I wanted it. I was ready for anything and everything that God wanted to do. And I couldn't believe that Cindy and Laura had turned him down.

Ray looked at Darrell who was standing just behind my right shoulder. I looked back at him also, and he seemed as uneasy as a boy who'd just been caught stealing a candy bar. The silence stretched like a rubber band till I broke it. "What?" I asked too loudly.

Ray answered, "It seems as though Darrell is uncomfortable with the idea, and since he's your husband and spiritual head, I'm not going to go against his wishes. Am I right?"

Darrell nodded. This was a situation I hadn't expected, and I didn't have the energy or the words to argue at the moment. As I looked from one of them to the other, I couldn't quite get past the fact that Darrell, Cindy and Laura had all turned Ray down. To my mind, they had rationalized themselves out of spiritual help. I thought they were nuts. Then I wondered why I thought I needed something more and they didn't. My living room seemed like a closed clubhouse, and I was left standing alone outside the door.

Ray interrupted my thoughts, "I have some intercessors at home that I need to talk to. I need to tell them that they're not praying for the baptism with the Holy Spirit, but to continue to pray for the cleansing. May I use your phone?"

Darrell took Ray into the kitchen to the telephone on the wall.

The three of us women talked while he was in the other room. Cindy said in way of explanation, "Bruce was a basket case when I left to come here. I just don't think it's right for me to do this tonight—maybe later. It's not that I don't need it or want it though."

Laura said, "I just don't think I'm ready for that. I'm just not sure…"

I kept silent; I didn't know what to say. I was so needy at the moment that I was willing to receive anything Ray had to offer, and it didn't matter to me that I didn't understand everything about the baptism with the Holy Spirit. I was also irritated at Darrell for effectively stopping Ray from praying for me.

Ray came bustling back into the room and said, "If you don't mind, I'd like to pray over you." He reached into his pocket, took out a small vial of oil and opened it. Tipping it over his thumb, he made the sign of the cross on Laura's forehead, then placed his hand on her head and asked the Lord to anoint her for the task of ministering to Tammy. He also prayed in tongues—something I'd never heard before. He did the same for Cindy and then for me. No one questioned the praying in tongues, so I kept my mouth shut also. I didn't quite know what to make of it, but it didn't seem to bother me either. My mind was beginning to calm down after the storm of the last 24 hours.

"I asked that we meet at your house," Ray continued looking pointedly at Darrell and I, "because Tammy spent the night here and she's ridden in your car. When someone is possessed or oppressed by demons, they carry an entourage around with them. It's sort of like having a cold. When you sneeze, germs fly out and land on everything around you, and they can infect other people and make them sick, too."

He paused to let that concept sink in.

Ray had just shined a flashlight under the rock, and the bugs were scuttling about, running for darkness. He'd just stirred up the image of the snake pit that was my downstairs level in my mind, and I instinctively hugged myself. Any calm I'd started to feel just flew out the window, and fear slithered back in. My skin crawled with unseen vipers and rattlers. I wanted to jump out of my seat and scream and smack my arms all over my body, killing anything that clung to me. I wanted to cry. This was too much for me to take.

"That must be why I felt the way I did," I said, somehow maintaining a serene facade.

"What do you mean?" asked Ray.

"I had to wash all that Tammy slept on or wore; everything seemed dirty. I would normally wash the linens, but this seemed different—so unclean that I could barely stomach touching them—like they'd leave cooties on me. They're down in the dryer right now. I dreaded going downstairs to my own family room. I thought maybe I'd see demons flying at me or crawling out from under the hide-a-bed. I just felt dirty."

Ray nodded. I looked at Cindy and Laura. Nobody thought I was over-the-edge weird. They all seemed to understand.

"I felt uncomfortable at school all by myself," Laura said.

"Usually I'm fine, but I was jumping at every sound I heard and always looking over my shoulder. That's why I called Ray."

Cindy added, "I know how you feel. I couldn't sit still at home. I kept scratching my head as though something was crawling in my hair. I felt like I had to wipe the whole day off me somehow."

"So what do we do about it?" Darrell asked, ever the practical male.

"That's why I came over. I wanted to help you take care of the problem. We're going to do a cleansing of your house, your van and the three of you," Ray answered, pointing to the women. "I see you have a cross on the wall, but do you happen to have a crucifix, even a small necklace?"

"No, we don't. Just the cross," I answered. "Why would you want a crucifix?"

"Satan hates the crucifix; it's a reminder of Jesus dying for our sins. But the cross will do. Mind if I take it off the wall and use it?" Ray asked, already up and moving towards the wall at the top of the stairs where the simple wood and metal cross hung.

"Go ahead," I answered. We were all up on our feet and ready for action even though none of us knew what he was going to do next.

"We're going to pray over your house room by room. We'll start up here towards the back of the house, pray over a room, then close the door and move on to the next room."

Darrell led him to our bedroom and we all crowded in. I didn't care what my house looked like at the moment—unmade bed, a few clothes scattered about, toys on the floors, dishes unwashed—I made no apologies. All pride evaporated; I just wanted to get rid of any demons lurking around my house.

Ray lifted the cross above his head and began praying, "Jesus, we exalt You. You are the Most High God, the Lord of all, Lord of Heaven and Earth. We claim this house for you, Lord Jesus.

We pray your blood over this house and ourselves for protection against the evil one. By the power and authority that You give to all who believe in Your name, we come against Satan and all his evil demons. We command you out of this room in Jesus name!"

Ray's commanding voice and forceful prayer seemed to wash over the room like a tidal wave, taking any evil that was lurking right along with it. Then he ushered us out of that room, closed the door behind him and led us into the adjacent spare bedroom/sewing room. He lifted the cross again and commanded any demons to leave that room, then we left, closing the door behind us. He repeated the process in every room upstairs, opening the front door and commanding demons to exit the house. The process and Ray's boldness began to strengthen my weary spirit. Though none of us were quite as loud and bold as Ray, we all started praying along with him.

He led us downstairs, and since the kids were asleep in the two bedrooms, he quietly opened their doors and prayed before shutting them again. We prayed over the bathroom, the laundry room where the items were done tossing in the dryer, and then Ray vehemently ordered all demons out the sliding glass door as he prayed over our family room. He ended the prayer down there and declared the house cleansed. I felt a sense of relief, but the job wasn't done yet.

We moved outside to the driveway where my blue minivan still sat. We opened every door, circled the van and Ray held the cross high inside and prayed it clean of vermin.

We all trooped back inside and up the stairs. "Now we're going to pray over you all," Ray said. One at a time, he held the cross over each of us and prayed against any demons clinging to us or trying to harass or oppress us.

Afterwards we held hands in our circle, and Ray prayed for all sorts of things for us—a good night's sleep, boldness in witness, fluency in our prayers, understanding of the Bible, strength to stand up against the evil one, the comfort and power of the Holy Spirit.

And then he was done and saying good-bye. We'd learned so much from Ray that it was difficult to process it all in those two short hours. None of us had ever experienced anything close to what had happened to us that evening. Just as evil enveloped Tammy's apartment that afternoon, God's holy presence fell on us in my living room like the gentle rain outside wet the ground. Before Ray came, I was in panic mode, feeling anxious and dirty. Now I was calm, comforted and clean. We tried to thank him, but didn't have words large enough to convey our gratefulness. He'd generously offered his time to pray for us, and his kindness overwhelmed me. This rather blustery, bold man seemed like a big teddy bear, and shy as I was, I impulsively hugged him good-bye.

First Ray left, and shortly after, Laura and Cindy dashed out with jackets over their heads to stay dry. Darrell and I went quietly to bed, and I slept like a cat stretching out in the morning sunbeam, oblivious and not caring what the next day would bring. For now, I was at peace.

Chapter Seven
SMASHING BOXES

I pray also that the eyes of your heart may be enlightened in order that you may know the hope to which he has called you, the riches of his glorious inheritance in the saints, and his incomparably great power for us who believe.
Ephesians 1:18-19a

"How are you doing this morning?" I asked Cindy over the phone. It was 10:00 Monday morning when I decided to take a break from my Bible reading.

"I'm all right, I guess. How about you?" Cindy asked.

"Well, I slept great last night, but once I sent my older two children off to school, yesterday's fears started creeping up on me, so I've been reading my Bible. That helped me a bit. I don't feel dirty anymore or feel like my house is infected with demons, but I can't stop thinking about Tammy and rehashing yesterday afternoon in my mind," I said as I roamed the kitchen putting away the morning cereal boxes and loading the dishwasher.

"I've thought about her myself. What do you suppose she's doing today?"

"I don't know. Every time I think about her, I get scared again."

"I keep imagining her talking to Jan and telling her all about us, and then Jan having a meeting with her coven of witches and putting a curse or spell on us," Cindy said.

"Or asking Satan to break our legs or kill us, right?" I asked. I could almost hear Cindy's fear matching my own through the telephone.

"And what about our families? Do you think they could get hurt?"

"Gosh, Cindy, I hadn't thought of that one yet. I'm starting to freak out now," I said, peeking around the wall separating the kitchen from the living room to see if Rachel was still playing in there.

"Sorry. I guess I'm getting carried away, but there's so much we don't know yet. I wish we'd thought of these questions last night; we could have asked Ray."

"You know, when I take Rachel to preschool this afternoon, I can ask Laura for Ray's phone number. We can call and ask him about curses and spells and anything else we think of."

"You want to come over here while Rachel's at preschool? Keri and Tim will be napping, so we can talk and pray," Cindy said.

"Actually, yes, I'd love to come over. I hate to admit it, but I hate being home alone right now. I've even kept Rachel up here playing this morning rather than letting her play downstairs. I think the unknown is what's scaring me."

"Okay then, what time do you think you'll be here—12:45?"

"Yeah, I should be there by then. Have you started reading your Bible yet this morning? I just began reading in the New Testament to see what I find that will shed some light on both the occult and the Holy Spirit like that guy told us to."

"I've already started in Acts, and I'm taking notes," Cindy said.

"Good idea," I said sliding open a drawer in my desk beside

the kitchen counter and rummaging for a notebook. "I'll see you this afternoon then. Bye."

The rest of the morning blurred by like a jet's exhaust. I sat on the couch cross-legged, Bible on my lap, pen in hand and notebook beside me. Rachel played quietly nearby, barely noticed by me. So long as she had me within view, she seemed content to play alone with her dollies. I started reading in Acts, like Cindy had, figuring that we could discuss what we learned that afternoon. I'd read my Bible for the ladies' Bible study group I was in every Wednesday, but I wasn't in the habit of reading it every day or reading it for more than an hour and a half straight. Before I realized it, I was late making our lunch and getting Rachel ready for preschool.

We hurried through our peanut butter sandwiches, changed her clothes, brushed her dark brown hair into two ponytails and I seat belted her into the van. All the way to school, I did something very strange, for me; I prayed. I prayed as easily as turning on the faucet and letting water pour out. Up to this point, my prayers were short with stunted sentences. I prayed like one with a stutter, never seeming to get very far in my conversations with God. It had been a lack in my spiritual life that left me at a loss as to how to fix it. I just couldn't think of enough stuff to pray about to keep me going for more than five minutes. But now, I was praying naturally, not even thinking about what to pray for next—the thoughts were just there like turning the next page in the book.

I didn't have time to give this newfound ability much thought at the moment as I arrived in the school/church parking lot, then entered the building with Rachel. After depositing her in the classroom, I turned to Laura's touch on my shoulder.

"Hi, Rhonda. How are you doing today?" She was standing alongside an unfamiliar man dressed in a suit.

"I'm fine. Better than last night anyway. How are you?"

"I'm OK. Keeping busy has helped. Rhonda, I'd like you to meet someone. This is Pastor Jim. He's a pastor from the same church where Ray works."

We shook hands and exchanged nice-to-meet-you's.

"He just happened to drop by today, and I've been talking to him for the last half hour about Tammy and what went on yesterday. He's been able to answer a few of my questions; I bet you have some of your own. I have to get into the classroom, but Jim said he'd stay and talk to you if you need to."

With that she slipped by me into her classroom and began hugging and greeting the preschoolers. Jim and I stood facing each other in the hallway.

"Do you mind talking with me?" I asked. He said "no," and I gestured him over to the other side of the hallway out of the lane of traffic in and opposite the preschool doorway. Then I began by bombarding him with the question topmost on my mind—"Can Tammy and her witch friends bring a curse or cast a spell against us and our families?"

"No," he said. "Well, they can, but they won't if they know you're Christians. Anything they try to do to you would come back to them double, so witches don't usually try to curse Christians because they know it will backfire. You don't need to be afraid of them." He put his hand on my shoulder and looked right into my eyes. Obviously he could see some lingering fear residing there.

"I guess I am afraid of them," I admitted. "This is all so new to me. One minute, I'll be doing okay, then the next moment, I'll be overwhelmed with fear."

"Let's pray about it." And right then and there he began praying to God to lift the fear off me. His prayer lasted about five minutes, but I felt a little conspicuous bowing in prayer in the hallway of my church's school. It wasn't a common sight outside the bounds of the sanctuary on Sunday mornings, and even then we prayed only when told to. Nobody just erupted in prayer in the middle of the hallway. But need surpassed vanity, and I took in every word, letting his prayer soak into my spirit like lotion rubbed on dry skin.

"Thank you. You don't even know me, and here you are taking time out of your day to pray for me." I was very humbled by these people spending time on what I viewed as my problems.

"This is what people of the Kingdom do for each other. Do you have any other questions for me?"

"I can't think of any right now, but I probably will after you leave," I laughed.

He took a small notebook out of his pocket and wrote on it before handing it to me. "I'm a little difficult to reach during the day, but if you have any more questions, I want you to feel free to call me at home in the evening. I put my wife's name, Anne, on there. I'm going to tell her about you, and if you need someone to pray with you, if fear becomes a problem again, anytime during the day—please call her."

"I couldn't do that. She's never even met me!"

"You can do it," Jim said. "She will be happy to pray with you over the phone if you need her to. She's very knowledgeable about these subjects and has the gift of intercession." He hesitated, cocking his head to one side, "You know you need to call this girl again, don't you?"

"You mean Tammy? I don't want to call her," I blurted, shaking my head.

"When we were praying, I had a sense from God that you were supposed to call her. God has appointed *you* to call her," he said pointing to me for emphasis.

I crossed my arms in front of my chest and looked away. "I was afraid of that. I felt God nudging me to call her this morning, but I ignored it," I said looking back at Jim. "I'm not ready."

"You don't have to call her today, but you need to call her soon. Let God take care of the fear and show you what to say to her. I've got to go now, but call me or Anne if you need us, okay?"

"Okay." He waved and was out the door as I stood immobile in the hallway for a few minutes marveling at the help we were receiving from friends and strangers alike. Then I remembered that I'd told Cindy I'd be at her house by 12:45, and it was already that time. I went to the parking lot, got in my car and headed north towards Cindy's. Again, I prayed the whole way there without thinking. Prayers flowed out loud as though I were carrying on an earnest conversation with an invisible person in the seat next to me.

After sharing what I'd learned from Pastor Jim in the hallway at school, Cindy and I sat down at her kitchen table and discussed Acts. We'd both been taking similar notes and needed to chew them over together.

Cindy said, "I feel as though I've never read Acts before. I'm gaining so much from it. I wonder how come I've never noticed all the references to the Holy Spirit before. Did you notice the words 'baptized with the Holy Spirit' and 'filled with the Holy Spirit'? I think I'm going to keep track of those passages. Also, I don't remember being taught anything on speaking in tongues, visions, dreams, or prophecy."

"I'm not sure I've ever read Acts all the way through. There's a lot here that I've never heard a sermon on or studied in a Bible study before. How come do you suppose?" I asked.

"It's controversial. I don't think people know what to do with these things, so passages that deal with them are either ignored or glossed over, saying those things aren't for today."

"Do you think tongues, visions and prophecy are for us today?"

"I don't know yet, but it sure seems like it. If they are for today, I'm going to have to rethink what I've been taught. I've heard of people who speak in tongues and just thought they were weird. I do know that I'm going to study it, though. Look, it's raining again," Cindy said pointing. I turned in my seat at her kitchen table to look out the window and saw the gentle drizzle dampening the driveway and my van.

Cindy went to check on her kids, and we settled down on the couch to talk some more. We discussed Pastor Jim's remark about me calling Tammy and all the possible ways that Tammy would react to my reaching out to her again. We laid all of our fears and feelings bare, relieved to find that we thought and felt similarly. Then we prayed.

Normally, I was shy about praying out loud—especially in front of people who prayed "better" than I. Cindy was an eloquent prayer; words flowed easily like a river knowing its path. I was embarrassed by my lack of words, and my prayers were more like a dammed-up creek. But a peace about praying with Cindy descended on me; I was outgrowing my old spiritual bounds by the minute. The dam burst and the creek ran freely— I prayed whatever was on my mind and heart. And there was a lot to pray about! We prayed easily for half an hour. The current took us around one bend then another until it was time for me to pick up Rachel from preschool.

We stood on her side porch a moment watching the sprinkling rain, but it stopped just as I needed to leave. I prayed quietly on my way to the school and then again returning home.

Two phenomena occurred repeatedly over the next several weeks—rain fell whenever Cindy and I prayed together, and every time I drove my van, I prayed without ceasing.

Cindy and I dubbed the van "my blue chariot." I relished the sensation of communing with God on all the subjects that He placed on my heart. Together we traveled the byways of the city and the roadways of heaven. Every mountain had a pass, every river a bridge. My spirit revved with joy every time I entered my blue chariot. Never before was prayer a two-way street; it was always one-way, with me unsure if I was going the right way. For the first time, prayer became a wide highway instead of a narrow road filled with potholes.

I didn't stop to think of the right words to say in just the right order, never leaving first gear. Now I zoomed in fifth gear whenever I drove, not worrying about changing gears or having enough gas. Before, I'd been criticized for not praying properly, not using ACTS as a guide—adoration, confession, thanksgiving, supplication. I'd also been frowned at if I forgot the rote, "in Jesus' name" at the end. Now my worries about praying properly flew out the window as I concentrated on God alone. This newly found freedom in prayer transcended the chariot and moved into every area of my life. I was no longer awkward praying aloud by myself or with others, nor did I run out of subjects. Now I ran out of time.

The rain seemed a magical event when Cindy and I came together in prayer. Sometimes I wondered if the heavens showered only over the house where we met. I'd drive the half mile home and notice that my block was dry. Most often, the rain delicately drizzled, but occasionally the clouds wrung themselves dry in a downpour. When our prayers were focused on spiritual warfare, the sky crackled with electricity and booming thunder. God was placing His signature all over our prayers. He stamped His approval and validated us. Once in a while, we stood out in the rain, arms flung wide to receive Him. We would allow the shower to moisten our skin and clothing as God soaked our spirits, cleansing and feeding them. As fall slipped into winter, it became too cold to rain, so it snowed.

Every day that week and for several weeks following, both Cindy and I had new routines that included six to eight hours a day of reading—mostly scripture. Somehow we managed to tend to our children, husbands and households. We devoured our Bibles as the Israelites their manna.

Although I'd been a Christian for twelve years now and had been involved in weekly ladies' Bible studies and Sunday morning Bible studies, I was widening my knowledge base on the Holy Spirit daily. Previously, I remembered hearing that the Holy Spirit brings us to faith and gives us gifts, but that teaching seemed to be the end of the line, not the beginning. I didn't even remember a sermon based solely on the work of the Holy Spirit, nor had I ever had a Bible lesson on Him. Vaguely, I remembered celebrating Pentecost. Now I feasted on what happened to the people after the Holy Spirit fell with power on that Pentecost so long ago. And I began to desire my own Pentecost.

What was this power all about anyway? I delved deeper into the Word to find out, and every time I came up for air, I pondered what I'd learned. And I smashed my tiny "God box." I'd always placed God in this tiny package and neatly tied it with ribbon to keep Him securely stuffed and presentable.

On Tuesday after my reading, I untied the ribbon and ripped apart the box. My God didn't fit there anymore. Power can't be boxed. I wasn't in the habit of kneeling in prayer, but that day I slid off the couch and onto the floor. The realization of a huge God compared to puny me brought me to my knees asking God to forgive me for my attempt to box Him up. Kneeling became habitual; I couldn't seem to keep myself seated in His presence. Then the carpet demanded my attention as I lay prostrate before this awesome God I was just beginning to fathom.

As I continued to study the person of the Holy Spirit, I read that He could be lied to (Acts 5:3-4) and grieved (Eph. 4:30). I'd thought of Him as some wispy thing before, but now I realized He was indeed a person. I discovered why the Holy Spirit was given (John 14:16-18, 16:7). Jesus didn't want to leave us as orphans, so he gave us the Holy Spirit to be in us and with us forever. I was awed by the fact that Jesus considered it better that He leave and return to heaven because He was sending the Holy Spirit. It seemed that Jesus viewed the Holy Spirit as highly important to us, so why didn't I hear more about Him?

I pored over John 14 through 16 and made a list of all the ways the Holy Spirit helps me in my everyday life. He is my Counselor; He teaches me all things; He reminds me of Jesus' words; He testifies to me about Jesus; He will help me testify about Jesus; He guides me into all truth; He will tell me what is yet to come; He makes Jesus and His words known to me.

Reading Romans 5, 8 and 15 made my list longer. There is so much that the Holy Spirit does for me—God shows His love for me through the Holy Spirit; I am set free from condemnation; He makes us God's children and heirs; He helps me in my weakness; He searches my heart; He intercedes for me, prays the deep things of my heart to God, the Father; He gives me hope; He sanctifies me; He empowers me to perform signs and miracles. I learned so many new teachings about the Holy Spirit. How had I bypassed all this information before?

Daily, my beliefs changed and expanded until they broke out of my own little theological boxes. I read further about miracles and spiritual gifts, and I no longer believed that miracles were not for believers today. After all, I had experienced a few miracles in the few short weeks that I'd known Tammy. Spiritual gifts fascinated me as I noticed the early Christians using them. I decided that they also were for believers to use today and began wondering what my gifts were. I also wondered why I was never taught these things before. The rich greenhouse of the Bible was being opened before me, and I entered and rooted myself in its soil. And I outgrew my box.

I visited Northwestern Bookstore, a local Christian bookstore, for the first time on Wednesday and discovered Christian music and books. I bought books on the occult, the Holy Spirit and spiritual gifts. Standing in front of the array of albums, I asked God to pick out the music for me; then I took home Michael W. Smith, Keith Green, Amy Grant and Twila Paris. I found the local Christian radio station—KTIS—and tuned in on a daily basis. I immersed myself and surrounded myself with God and all things Christian. Every waking moment was filled with Him, and it was a glorious honeymoon.

The phone lines buzzed underground along the half-mile route between Cindy's house and mine. As I was smashing my own boxes, Cindy found the theology she had been taught from grade school through college to be too limiting. While I suffered the ailment of lack, she suffered the disease of doubt. The teaching she'd received placed doubt and caution in her mind rather than awe and freedom. I found filling the void easier than Cindy found replacing the restraints of her theology. Every day was an adventure in the Bible filled with new teachings and discoveries that we shared with each other.

Parallel to learning about the Holy Spirit was absorbing knowledge about the occult through the Bible and Christian books. Reading about the occult drove me to needing God and prayer; I could only digest so much evil and wickedness at a time. Gaining knowledge had a way of making me feel even more ignorant than before. Every book and every passage brought me closer to the realization that dabbling in the occult was serious business with God. I was exploring a whole new ugly world and realizing just how uneducated, naïve and inept I was. And I recognized how Tammy's deep involvement had bound her to

Satan and brought about the revolting manifestations we'd become spectators to. This new perception did not endear me to Tammy; it further tore open the seam that she'd started ripping that Sunday.

But seams are repairable if God wants them mended, and God continued to nudge me to finish what He'd started. I *had* to call Tammy. The choice before me was clear—take myself out of God's will or stay the path and contact Tammy. I decided to call her. But first, I needed a little bit more information from a live person rather than a book.

I phoned Pastor Jim. Even though it was difficult to phone a near stranger, need superceded shyness, and on Thursday night the same week of that Sunday, I reached him.

"What do I do with Tammy once I call her?" I asked. I had pen in hand ready to take notes; I'd decided to follow his instructions or write down any wisdom he uttered. "Should the goal still be to take her to church?"

"Well, bringing her to church is a start, but what she really needs is a deliverance. You're going to have to ask her if she wants to be free from her occult bondage," he said.

"So, if she says she wants deliverance, then what do I do? I don't know how to do one. I've read a little about it, but there's no way I could do it by myself or even with Cindy."

"There's a pastor at our church who has a deliverance ministry. He sees people on Tuesday and Thursday mornings, and you can make an appointment for Tammy to see him. Hold on; I'll get the phone number for you."

While I was waiting for him to come back, my imagination moved forward a few steps. First of all, I couldn't imagine a person doing deliverance on a biweekly basis. I thought I'd seen enough in one afternoon to last me a lifetime. Then I saw us bringing Tammy to the church and sitting, waiting our turn in a room full of people like her—people who fell on the floor in a seizure. Or they could be even worse than Tammy—perhaps screaming and vomiting and who knew what else. These thoughts made me shudder.

Pastor Jim came back and recited the number, and then he prayed with me over the phone so that I would have the courage to call Tammy the next day and allow the Holy Spirit to give me the words to say to her.

After hanging up the phone, I had a new resolve to carry through with God's plan for Tammy. But I decided to wait until tomorrow. I'd been honeymooning with God for four days and wasn't quite ready to let Tammy's occultic displays intrude into my life again. Tomorrow would be soon enough.

I didn't realize that the enemy thought tomorrow would be too soon.

Chapter Eight
HOLY SPIRIT POWER

But you will receive power when the Holy Spirit comes on you; and you will be my witnesses in Jerusalem, and in all Judea and Samaria, and to the ends of the earth.
Acts 1:8

I awoke with a start. *What was that? Did I hear something, or was I just dreaming?* I lay completely still, listening in the dark for several moments, eyes wide open and breathing shallowly. When my eyes adjusted to the dark, I stared at the doorway to our bedroom. It was still closed and nothing in the room seemed amiss. Slowly I rolled over onto my back. Darrell was facing me and breathing evenly. Still listening for something that I thought woke me up, I lay stiff as a corpse for several minutes.

I heard nothing, but the heaviness in the room felt like the ceiling pressing down on me in bed. It seemed as though someone was crouching in the room waiting to pounce on me. *It's nothing. There's no one here. Go back to sleep.* I tried talking myself out of paranoia.

Then I looked down at the foot of the bed. A dark presence stood there, and I gasped and covered my mouth with my hand.

I wanted to run screaming out of the room, but I dared not move. The black presence had bodily form but no discernable features; it didn't move. Evil emanated from it so palpable that it seemed to have substance like a thick, dark cloud engulfing me. I could barely breathe. Fear immobilized me. I squeezed my eyes closed hoping I was dreaming and it would disappear.

It didn't.

Jesus. Jesus. Jesus. It's all I could think in my frozen mind. The presence didn't budge. What was this thing? Was it a ghost? A demon? Satan himself? My mind whirled with possibilities, but clearly I'd been unprepared for this apparition at the foot of my own bed. *Jesus, make it go away!* Still there. *Jesus, help me!*

The answer came, and I sat up in bed and spoke out loud, "Jesus, Jesus, Jesus." Over and over I repeatedly whispered His name like a mantra getting louder and more authoritative each time until the presence evaporated like fog before my eyes. My heart was pounding so hard and fast that I thought surely it would wake Darrell even if my speaking aloud hadn't. He was sleeping soundly and hadn't budged. I plopped back onto my pillow and prayed—a little more fluently now—for what seemed like an hour.

Slowly my breathing normalized and my heart beat quietly. My tense body relaxed. Fear crept out and sleep eased in and covered me like a warm blanket.

After getting Derek and Dawn off to the school bus the next morning, the fears of the night before settled in again and threatened to stick to me like chewing gum to the bottom of a shoe. I'd resolved to call Tammy this morning, but after the visitation during the night, I no more wanted to talk to her than I wanted to pet a snake. She was the cause of my fears. She was the reason for that presence at the foot of my bed.

As I blamed her for all that ailed me, I also began to realize that Satan was trying to keep me away from Tammy by keeping me bound in fear. I got mad and decided to do something about it. I marched over to my refrigerator and took down the piece of paper from Pastor Jim that I'd stuck under a magnet. I would call his wife, Anne.

I dialed hurriedly, and after introductions, she pushed my apologies aside and shot straight to the heart of the matter. "What do you need me to pray for right now?"

I took an immediate liking to this no-nonsense woman. "I was going to call Tammy this morning, but I'm afraid." I explained what went on in my bedroom last night.

Anne said, "You're right. Satan is trying to stop you from ministering to this girl, and he'll use any tricks he can to keep you inactive. Most likely that was a demon in your bedroom last night. You did the right thing, though, by using Jesus' name out loud."

Then she immediately lapsed into prayer. "Lord, we honor you. You alone are worthy of our praise. You know the situation with Rhonda and Tammy, and we ask for your intervention right now. Rhonda is going to call Tammy, and I pray that you would give her the courage she needs to do so. Satan, we bind you right now in Jesus' name. We bind your use of fear to scare Rhonda away from ministering to Tammy. Leave her alone. You have no right to harass her; she belongs to Jesus. So be gone in Jesus' name! Lord, I pray that you would cover Rhonda with your blood and protect her in all her dealings with Tammy. Strengthen and build her up as she lives her daily life. Amen."

"Wow. That was some powerful praying! No one has ever prayed for me quite like that before. Thank you."

"No thanks needed. Call me again if you need more prayer. I'm happy to trounce on Satan any chance I get," she chuckled.

"I will call you again. And really, thanks. I don't feel afraid anymore, and I'm going to call Tammy as soon as I hang up." I hung up the phone, checked on Rachel playing school with her dolls in the living room then immediately dialed Tammy's number.

"Hello?"

"Tammy, this is Rhonda."

"Rhonda! I haven't heard from you all week. Why haven't you called?"

"Well," I hesitated, "I wasn't sure you'd want to hear from me again."

"Why?" She sounded innocently flabbergasted by my statement.

"After last Sunday…" I didn't quite know how to continue.

"You came over to help me get rid of all my occult stuff. You must have done it because I haven't seen any of it around here. I had a lot of seizures that day, didn't I? I can barely remember what happened when you were here."

This was a turn I hadn't expected. I sat down hard at the dining room table. *How can she possibly not remember what happened?*

"Tammy, do you remember Cindy, Laura and I coming to your apartment and gathering your occult stuff in a grocery bag?"

"I remember getting in the car with you guys to come here. I sort of remember you being here, but that's about it."

"That's not very much! We were there all afternoon. Do you remember three other people coming to your apartment to help us?"

"No, why would you need help?"

She sounded like the Tammy I knew before that Sunday—so harmless, so genuine. I took a deep breath and decided to plunge in and explain what happened at her apartment that day. "Tammy, you weren't yourself that afternoon. You had a lot of seizures, and you weren't very helpful when we were gathering the occult stuff. Well, you started out helpful, but then you decided you wanted some of it back—like your Ouija Board." I touched on the rest of the story, leaving out some of the grisly details but telling her of her violence towards the one visitor.

Silence. "Are you there, Tammy?"

"Yes," came the barely audible voice through the phone lines. "I'm so sorry. I must have been awful. I don't even remember." She was crying, her voice catching in sobs.

"It's all right, Tammy. Cindy and I are still willing to work with you, and we're going to get you some help. There's a pastor at a church nearby who has a deliverance ministry. We can make an appointment with him for you, if you want to be free from the occult."

"I'll go, if you think that's what I should do."

"I do, Tammy. Cindy and I really don't know how to help you. You need someone who knows something about this kind of thing. We'll make an appointment for you and then get back to you."

I hung up feeling both relieved and encouraged—the phone call had gone better than I'd thought it would, and Tammy was willing to get help. In all our imaginings about Tammy's reaction after that Sunday, it never occurred to us that she wouldn't remember what went on.

I stopped by Cindy's house while Rachel was at preschool that afternoon and told her about my night visitation and phone calls. I brought along the phone number to call for an appointment for Tammy, and Cindy made the call.

"Can you believe it?" she said. "They're booked up for two weeks! I asked for one sooner, but I had to make the appointment for two weeks from now!"

"You mean there are that many people who need deliverance? I can't imagine. What are we going to do with Tammy for two more weeks?"

"I don't know."

We discussed how we should best proceed with Tammy, then we prayed and watched the rain fall. I stayed until it was time to pick Rachel up again.

During the following weeks, we continued to minister to Tammy, but we also had help. An older couple at our church volunteered to chauffeur Tammy to church and other appointments. Pastor Ken and Nancy also saw Tammy regularly, easing the burden of our daily contacts with her. Tammy seemed to be soaking up Jesus during this time; she was an eager learner. She was in and out of various hospitals for one reason or another. Because of her frequent seizures, her doctor decided to run more tests and monitor her seizures. But she never got any better despite changes in medications.

Even though we were waiting for Tammy's appointment day to arrive, Cindy and I were not idle. We continued our frenzy of absorbing the Bible, Christian books and music. And we were growing spiritually stronger every day. We asked God question after question and found the answers in His Word. No human was our teacher during this time, but only our heavenly Father, and He taught us well.

The more we learned about the Holy Spirit, the more we saw the lack of power in our own lives, and the more we wanted of God. Ministering to Tammy continually depleted us physically and spiritually, so we began to ask God to fill us up.

As I studied the Bible, I was beginning to form a picture in my mind about who the Holy Spirit was and what He does in a believer's life. I saw in John 20:22 that Jesus "breathed on them and said, 'Receive the Holy Spirit.'" Then in Acts 1:4-5 Jesus commanded them: "Do not leave Jerusalem, but wait for the gift my Father promised, which you heard me speak about. For John baptized with water, but in a few days you will be baptized with the Holy Spirit." Jesus continued in verse 8: "But you will receive power when the Holy Spirit comes on you; and you will be my witnesses in Jerusalem, and in all Judea and Samaria, and to the ends of the earth."

I'd always been taught, and it seemed true to scripture (Matthew 28:19), that when I was baptized, I'd received the Holy Spirit to live inside of me. I concluded that I indeed had the Holy Spirit residing in me because I was a believer. But was there a difference between water baptism and Holy Spirit baptism? After looking at instances in the Bible, I decided there was a difference. I saw a wimpy Peter before Acts 2, and a bold, on-fire Peter after being filled with the Holy Spirit in Acts 2:4. Acts has many instances where people were filled with the Holy Spirit, and the results of that filling were speaking in tongues, speaking the word of God boldly, praising God and performing miraculous signs and wonders.

After seeing what demons could do and having a taste of what God could do, I wanted more. I hungered for more of God; I thirsted to be filled to overflowing. Ministering to Tammy left me needing God as much as I needed food for my body. Everyday on my knees or on my face before God, I asked Him to fill me with His Holy Spirit, to baptize me with the Holy Spirit. I went from wanting the baptism to desiring it with my whole heart, then realizing that I needed it, and finally to begging God for it. I absolutely had to have it. It no longer seemed an option in my spiritual life, but an absolute must for every Christian.

Then one day in prayer, God gave me a vision. I saw before me a figure of a person sitting in a straight-backed wooden chair. His feet were bound to the front legs of the chair, his hands were tied behind his back and a cloth gagged his mouth and was tied in back of his head. "Who is this person?" I asked God. (I did not audibly speak, nor did I actually hear a voice, but it was as if I carried on a conversation with the unseen God in my vision.)

He replied, "This is the Holy Spirit in you. See, you have Him inside you, but He is tied up, bound and gagged. Every now and then you take the gag out of His mouth and untie His hands and feet, but when you've finished with Him, you return Him to the chair and bind and gag Him again until the next time you need His services."

"But Lord," I cried, "You're God. You can do anything! Why don't *You* untie and ungag Him?"

He answered me, "I do not force my way into your life. I have given the Holy Spirit freely, and this is how you treat Him. You must untie Him; you must take the gag out of His mouth. Then my Spirit will reign freely in your life as He is supposed to."

I threw myself on the floor in agony. I was guilty of binding the Holy Spirit in my life. I remembered times when I'd asked Him to help me, and He had. But then I forgot about Him until the next time. And He was God! How could I have treated God so shamefully? Remorse overwhelmed me and held me face down in the carpet.

With tears streaming unabated, I said, "Holy Spirit, I untie your feet so that You may take me places You want me to go. I untie Your hands so that You are free to work in me and through me. And I untie and take the gag out of Your mouth so that You may speak the Word of God boldly through me. I want you to roam freely in my life. I submit myself to You."

That was the turning point in my spiritual life. I had moved from comfortable to want to need. I was not ashamed to beg God to work in my life. I wanted everything, needed everything He had to offer. I emptied myself before Him as an offering. I gave Him all of me, all that I had, all that I was, all that I knew. I handed my life over to Him on a daily basis. I told God that whatever He wanted to do in my life, I would allow it, embrace it. I desired spiritual gifts to be evident in my life, and I told God I'd take any spiritual gift He wanted to grant me.

Even tongues. I didn't understand tongues, and I had little experience in that area other than knowing that Mary, who we'd called from Tammy's that Sunday, spoke in tongues, and we'd also heard Ray speak in tongues at my house that Sunday evening. But I decided that I couldn't hold back any part of myself from the Holy Spirit any longer, so I gave Him my tongue also.

As the appointment for Tammy's deliverance approached, Tammy ended up in the hospital again. So we made another appointment three weeks further down the road of this long pilgrimage. Cindy and I were walking down the same spiritual road; her journey mirrored mine except that hers was made for her personality and my trek was ordered to my own uniqueness.

Some five weeks after meeting Tammy, during the weekend of Cindy's birthday in October, we both had different experiences that took us down the same path.

Leading up to that weekend, Cindy's prayers had been similar to mine along the way, except that, though she'd had no teaching, she'd heard shady reports about people who spoke in tongues. And she wanted nothing to do with it. She'd asked God to do anything, give her anything—except tongues. But as she continued to pray, God had gently led her to the realization that He wanted all of her, not just part of her.

Kneeling by her bed one day, she asked God to baptize her with the Holy Spirit. Totally expectant, she waited, but in her heart she was hoping to *not* receive tongues. Until God gently spoke to her spirit, "I'm glad you believe Me, but if you don't trust me on one thing, it's the same as not trusting me on anything." Cindy groaned at the thought that she was shopping in His Kingdom, going down aisles picking and choosing what she wanted and leaving the rest. She thought that if she held back her tongue from Him, then she was keeping part of herself for herself, not willing to trust God with everything. God chiseled away until He broke through the wall, and she surrendered all.

After having read books on the subject, she decided she would follow their advice and try to speak in tongues—usually in the bathroom where she could be alone without interruption. She would start with *Jesus* then follow His name with syllables. As she heard her son Timmy in the living room playing with trucks and making noises, she repeated his sounds after *Jesus…ma…na.* She continued trying with no breakthrough until the weekend of her birthday.

As she was standing before the cutting board making sandwiches for a picnic with her children at a nearby park, she received a vision from God. There appeared a blackboard with what looked like three words written on it—foreign, strange words or syllables that she'd never seen before—ma nach tua. *This is very bizarre,* she thought.

She doubted in her heart that this was from the Lord, so she prayed, *Lord, if this isn't from you but is instead from the enemy, then take this blackboard and these words out of my mind. But if it is from you Lord, I pray that they would remain.* She opened her eyes and the blackboard, complete with the strange language, lingered.

She then sensed God nudging her to speak them out loud, but she decided to wait until she was at the park and her children were occupied on the playground. So she pushed the blackboard towards her peripheral vision, not wanting to look at it right then. But the vision stayed pasted there, hanging in midair. Sitting alone at the park while her children played on the equipment, she now hesitantly took a good look at her blackboard. She spoke the few chalked syllables aloud even though she felt silly doing so. No more words appeared nor did any other sounds come out of her mouth after those spoken.

Just three words. *Was this speaking in tongues? Surely there was more to it than this.* Again, she repeated the terms written on the invisible blackboard. *Okay, Lord, I said them aloud. I don't know what else to do.* The whole thing seemed strange, but she felt as though somehow she had made some progress that day in her obedience to God.

Immediately when she awoke the next morning, three additional words appeared on her blackboard. Starting from the beginning, she spoke them all aloud. She knew she had a full sentence, but had no clue what it meant. Again later, she asked God for more. Though the blackboard never reappeared, she spoke aloud new words as the Lord provided them, as much as her faith could handle. This continued for some time until she had two paragraphs of words and sentences that she recited. God gave enough manna for every day—all she could chew on—until she was hungry for more the next day.

The whole incident gave her great joy, a joy that bubbled up and spilled over and lasted. For a while, it was always the same words that she would repeat, but later we prayed about this gift and asked God to free her up in speaking in tongues, and He granted that freedom so that she could speak fluently in tongues.

Meanwhile, on that same weekend in October, I was home alone on Saturday; Darrell had taken the children out somewhere. I was sitting at my kitchen table surrounded by bills, and I began writing checks when a strange word popped into my head. It sounded like *shondola* with the accent on the first syllable. I recognized this word as one that Ray had spoken when he spoke in tongues. Why that one word stuck in my brain, I'll never know. But it repeated itself—over and over like a stuck needle on a record or a glitch on a tape. I ignored it as long as I could. After all, what was I going to do with it? Besides, I had bills to pay.

Finally, it became too obnoxious and insistent in my mind, so I said, yelled really, "Okay, I'll say it! *Shondola.*" Big deal. The heavens didn't open up. I heard no angels singing. I went back to my checkbook.

But God apparently wasn't finished with me. So I repeated the word again—and again. This time more syllables fell out of my mouth along with the word. Each time I said it, more syllables followed. And it was laughable. It sounded like baby talk, with stunted, short syllabic sounds. *Okay Lord, I did it. But surely this is not what speaking in tongues sounds like, is it?*

I tried to resume my task, but God intervened again. My mind was awash with sounds, and I could barely think. So I prayed, "Lord, I give up. If You want me to talk baby talk, I will. I'll do anything for You, You know that."

So I spoke some more, and was very glad that no one was there to hear me. Now a tune began to worm its way into my head— "Father I adore You." I sang this simple song in English first, then using my new syllables. Suddenly my sounds didn't seem quite so babyish anymore. They must have been real words with real meanings. And I crooned the whole song, over and again until my family returned.

It was difficult to control the joy that sprang forth like a new green plant when I sang my song. I smiled more frequently, laughed more readily and generally was easy to get along with. With God so in control of my life, I worried less.

It was a few months before I actually moved from singing in tongues to speaking in tongues. Cindy and I prayed for freedom in my language also—with the same results.

Even though our experiences happened the same weekend, neither of us was willing to spill forth her story. Somehow, each of us thought the other might not understand or perhaps laugh. After a week though, we couldn't stay bottled up any longer. I'm not sure who fizzed out first, but it was a "Me too!" moment. We were in awe of how our experiences were similar, yet very different. We couldn't pinpoint the exact moment when God baptized us in the Holy Spirit, but we were sure that He had. No one laid hands on us and prayed over us. Nothing had been instantaneous. But somewhere, sometime during our journeys, God had answered our many fervent prayers and filled us up to overflowing.

Other results of being baptized in the Holy Spirit occurred regularly after that. Our worship time broke forth to new heights. We delighted in praising God tirelessly. The Bible was a living book that never ceased to strengthen and teach us. We learned so much as we continued to gobble up His Word. It was Bread and Life to us; we couldn't live without it. We began to speak out boldly at our church about our new experiences and growth—with mixed reactions. Some craved to hear what we had to say, some thought we were nuts, and others considered us a threat to their theology.

Our prayer times together and with others also took on new characteristics. We began to receive words of knowledge—a word from the Lord about which we couldn't possibly have known beforehand—and prayed accordingly. Our prayers were filled with wisdom from the Word of God as He taught us. God continued to give us visions for ourselves and for others that we prayed for. And we began to pray for healing—with positive results. God was no longer a sedate, wimpy God in our eyes. He was awesome and powerful, electric and dangerous. He performed miracles in the Bible, and we believed that He still could, so we prayed accordingly, asking for miracles. God had no limits; He moved freely outside our smashed boxes.

Remarks like, "God doesn't do that anymore," or "You shouldn't ask God for that," or "You should be careful," or "Those miracles could be the work of Satan" fell on deaf ears. We both knew that God indeed does miracles today. Scripture says that we should not be ignorant about and should desire spiritual gifts (1 Corinthians 12:1, 14:1) If Satan could perform miracles, I was sure that God could. I know that Satan mimics God, so his miracles and manifestations are mere images of what God can do. To say that God doesn't perform miracles anymore, but that Satan does is to take the power from God and attribute it to Satan. Isn't God more powerful after all? Scripture also says, "If you then, though you are evil, know how to give good gifts to your children, how much more will your Father in heaven give the Holy Spirit to those who ask him!" (Luke 11:13) I dared to ask God anything and everything, because I believed in His all-surpassing, amazing power. My God could do anything!

The most hurtful remarks were, "You think you have more of God than we do" or "You think you're better than us, don't you?" I didn't think that I had more of God than others; you either have Him or you don't, there's no in between. But I knew that now God had more of me than He'd ever had before. I knew that I'd relinquished parts of myself that I'd previously held back from Him. The baptism with the Holy Spirit didn't make me better than anyone else, just as being a believer didn't make me better than others. But being a believer gave me salvation, and being baptized with the Holy Spirit gave me fullness in the Lord that I'd never experienced before. I was positive that the baptism was for all Christians, not just some. And I was saddened when some wanted nothing to do with it—or me anymore, for that matter. But despite this sadness, God was so faithful to continually feed and fill me, and joy in Him superceded all sorrow or pain.

Our honeymoon period with God lasted for months. We enjoyed being in His presence as a bride adores her new husband. We panted after His every word. We longed for His touch. We danced in His arms. We protected our relationship by staying faithful. We thought of Him every waking minute—sometimes even dreaming of Him. He protected us, loved us, spent time with us, communed with us, gifted us. It was a match made in heaven.

Dealing with Tammy became easier, though still trying and energy sapping. We were better equipped to handle her seizures, to answer her spiritual questions. Our teaching became more real for her, yet more intense, and our prayers concerning her received visible results. She began to absorb the Bible and learn from it.

Yet every two steps forward met with one push back. She still needed deliverance. Even though we prayed with her and over her constantly as the days slipped into weeks, we knew that we were yet babes as far as deliverance was concerned. We still thought someone else could do better, and we waited impatiently for that magic day when Tammy would be delivered.

Chapter Nine
DELIVERANCE

And lead us not into temptation but deliver us from evil
Matthew 6:13

One week piled up onto the other like building blocks, but still Tammy continued to miss appointments because of hospitalizations. Like rocks falling off the edge of a cliff, we saw our hopes for Tammy's deliverance tumble down and smash at the bottom. It was now late November, and frustration mounted to the point of desperation; we *had* to get her to the next date for deliverance.

Our calendars were marked; we'd been heavily praying that Tammy would be well and available, but two days before the latest secured date, Tammy was again hospitalized—this time in Minneapolis.

Cindy called her there and reminded her of her appointment, but Tammy said she should be released the night before.

She tried calling Tammy at home the next evening, but there was no answer. So she called again at the hospital. Tammy was still there, but assured Cindy that her doctors would release her from the hospital in the morning so that she could make the meeting on time. It seemed nothing went smoothly where Tammy was involved. There was always a hitch. But this one seemed minor—surely she would be released in the morning.

We both made arrangements for our children the next day since we didn't want to take them along on this kind of trip. I drove, and we left early to pick up Tammy, arriving at the hospital an hour before she was due at the church. Cindy went in to get Tammy while I waited in my car in the front entrance drive. We decided that I would wait out front so that we wouldn't waste time parking in the garage across the street from the hospital. If I had to move the car, then I would just drive around the block and come back to the front entrance.

Cindy wandered around close to the entrance hunting for the elevator. Finally, she backtracked to the front desk to ask the receptionist which hallway to go down to find it. Following her directions, she arrived in front of a full, open elevator.

"There's room for one more," a lady motioned her on. When the elevator doors closed, she added, "We must have been waiting just for you. The elevator doors wouldn't close before you came."

Cindy thought that statement was a little strange, but stranger things than that had happened before. As they rose to the third floor, she sensed a heavenly escort next to her—a holy presence that calmed her nerves and buoyed her spirits. She'd been ushered into the elevator that had been held just for her. She felt she was on a mission that couldn't fail, and things were going nicely so far. This was it! It seemed as though the deliverance was actually going to happen.

When Cindy entered Tammy's room, Tammy was reclining on her bed and still in hospital gown and robe.

"Tammy, how come you're not dressed?"

"I haven't been released yet. The nurse said the doctors didn't sign my release forms."

Cindy sighed and crinkled her nose up. "I'll go back to the desk and find out why you haven't been released yet."

At the nurses' station she asked a nurse about Tammy's status. "Tammy was supposed to be released this morning so that we could take her to an appointment with a pastor. Can this be taken care of soon so that we can get her there on time?"

The nurse picked up Tammy's chart and flipped pages. "There's no way she's getting out anytime soon."

"Why?" Cindy asked trying not to be curt but drumming her nails on the counter in impatience.

"She needs three different doctors' signatures, and so far she has none. The likelihood of getting all three doctors to sign for her release within the next half hour is practically nil. I wouldn't count on getting her out of here this morning," she said, replacing Tammy's chart.

"Can't you call them and explain the situation?"

"No. These doctors could be anywhere. Even if I did reach them, it could take them awhile before they get here and sign her papers. I'm afraid there's just no way Tammy's going to be released right now."

Tammy was still lying in bed when Cindy came back to the room with her report.

"What are we supposed to do now?" Tammy asked scooting to the edge of her bed.

"We'll pray," Cindy stated firmly. Sitting down next to Tammy and holding her hands, Cindy began.

"Lord, You know the situation. Tammy has an appointment with Pastor Peterson soon, and she needs those signatures in order to be released. We know that you are a mighty God, and that you can arrange for those doctors to sign her release forms now. I come against any evil forces that are trying to keep Tammy from this deliverance in Jesus' name. Lord, we claim victory over this situation. It might look hopeless now, but I trust that you're going to get Tammy out of this hospital on time today so that she can meet with you at the church. Amen."

Silence expanded between them like a balloon as they stared at each other for a few minutes. Cindy's expectancy was high, and Tammy looked to her for the next move as a child trusting her parent.

Finally Tammy popped the inflated balloon. "Now what?" she asked.

"Well," said Cindy confidently, "Now we get your things together so that you can leave."

Without questioning her, Tammy set about packing her small overnight bag. Then there was a light rap on the door, and the nurse Cindy had talked to ten minutes ago at the desk opened the door to the room.

Frowning and seeming shocked, she said, "She can go now. Tammy has permission to leave."

"She has all three signatures?" Cindy asked.

"Yes. Not five minutes after you walked away from the desk, the doctors came by the nurse's station one by one and signed her release forms. She's free to go." Still looking somewhat incredulous, she handed Tammy her forms and then turned and left them alone.

"Wow." They both gaped. Then Cindy became all business. "Hurry up. Let's leave before they change their minds!"

Tammy bustled about gathering toiletries and stuffing them in her bag. She had put her sweat pants on underneath her hospital gown, but that's as far as she'd gotten before the nurse came with the news.

"Where's your coat?" Cindy asked

"I don't have one here. I only have a T-shirt."

"Just leave on the gown and robe then. They'll be warmer than the T-shirt. Let's go."

Cindy ushered Tammy down the hall, into the elevator and out the front doors into my waiting van. I'd been waiting over half an hour and had periodically had to drive around the block and come back so as not to tie up the space in front of the hospital entrance. But I had just pulled up when they hurried out of the front doors.

Tammy looked a bit comical in her sweat pants under the blue striped hospital gown and robe. Since Tammy had no coat along for the chilly weather, we wrapped her up as best we could in a plaid woolen blanket I found in the back of the van, and I flipped the heat up full blast. We'd have to hurry now in order to get to her appointment on time.

While I was waiting, I'd had plenty of time to worry and conjure up all sorts of scenarios. Now we were finally on our way, but underneath my excitement and expectation were also dread and fear of the unknown. My mind traveled ahead of me to the church where I imagined a waiting room full of people lined up in chairs against the wall, each with his or her own peculiar manifestations. Having seizures, foaming at the mouth, vomiting, screaming, wailing—I wasn't sure what to expect. Cindy and I had prayed on the way to the hospital, but I needed more, so I prayed silently. *Lord, give me strength to handle anything I see today.*

We found parking behind the church and entered the back door. Tammy seemed excited in the car on the way over, but as we were walking her down the long hallway towards the sanctuary, she went limp, and we struggled to lower her to the tile floor without dropping her. She began having a seizure right there in the hallway with us kneeling over her. We felt helpless in a strange place, but a man came around the corner and stopped to pray with us. A woman stepped out of a room and knelt beside us, adding her voice to ours. Soon we had a group of six surrounding Tammy, and the seizure stopped. I marveled at this place, these people taking the time to pray over a stranger, not asking questions, just knowing how to pray. I couldn't imagine this scene at my own church, where people would point and gawk and possibly back away.

The four people quietly went about their business, leaving us alone with her by the time she woke up. We helped her up and went down to the office to check in and fill out forms explaining the reason for the visit. There was no waiting room; we sat in the narthex. Everybody we met seemed normal. When it was our turn, we entered the sanctuary and started walking down the aisle, right towards the large cross hanging on the wood-paneled wall at the other end. The pastor and a female assistant waited up by the altar. Tammy began balking.

"I don't think I can do this. I think we should leave. I don't feel well. Maybe I can come back another time when I feel better."

"Now, Tammy. You're here; we should do this now. If you back out of this, I don't think we can help you anymore." I realized how forceful I was being, but I'd had it. It had already taken Herculean efforts and over a month to get her here; I wasn't about to have her give up that easily.

"Okay," she said in a small voice.

The three of us sat in the front pew with the pastor and his assistant facing us on folding chairs. Pastor Peterson was a small man with white tufts of hair looking a bit disarrayed. He was dressed in his clerical garb, white robe that fell down to his ankles, a large cross hanging front and center and a scarlet stole around his neck. He talked gently with Tammy for a while about her problems, and she seemed to ease out of the built-up tension into her cheery self. When he invited her to kneel at the altar, we knelt on either side of her. Pastor Peterson faced her on the other side of the railing and anointed her with oil on her forehead. "I anoint you in the name of the Father, and the Son and the Holy Spirit. Amen." And she collapsed backwards like a brick before we could grab hold of her. She began another seizure.

Pastor stood calmly looking around the sanctuary. He seemed oblivious to Tammy rolling and shaking on the floor at his feet. *I bet this happens to him every day.* "Do you feel the cold air?" he asked.

We nodded, turning our attention away from Tammy and back to him. A frigid breeze had swept across us as though gusting from an open door in January.

"We have company," he said looking up in the oak rafters and side to side in the church.

We followed his gaze, wondering what he meant. Cindy had a smile on her face and whispered, "Angels?"

"Demons," he said still gazing up around him. "Demons often fly in on a cold front. They're all over the place. Outside. There's hordes of them outside this building," he said sweeping his arm first to one side of the church then to the other. We peered up and listened as we heard the ceiling of the church creek and groan all around us. It was as though several heavy weights sat on it threatening to crash through. The sounds and icy draft made us both shudder.

How does he know there are demons here? Maybe it's just the wind. But a quick look outside told me there was little wind—only a slight swaying of the leafless trees. I looked up at this robed man, and my hesitation to believe him turned to respect.

Meanwhile, Tammy was writhing on the floor foaming at the mouth. Pastor Peterson's assistant was taking care of her, praying and wiping her mouth with a tissue. This was a bad seizure—her body shook vigorously on the carpeted floor.

Pastor knelt beside Tammy and prayed quietly over her for a while. Every now and then he'd stop as though listening. We prayed silently and listened attentively, hearing nothing but his droning voice and the creaking ceiling.

"She's clean," he announced. Then he commanded the seizure to stop. It did, and Tammy lay limp, sleeping on the carpet.

"She's clean," he repeated as he sat down in a folding chair and motioned us to sit in the front pew. He was so calm and casual about the whole scene before us. "I sense no demonic possession in her. Maybe she was possessed at one time. I wouldn't doubt it with all this activity surrounding her. She's definitely oppressed, though. She has an entourage of demons that follow her around. I'm sure they go with her wherever she goes. Satan isn't giving her up without a fight. She's got her work cut out for her; so do you if you're going to continue helping her." He smiled weakly as though he understood exactly what we'd been dealing with.

"Should we make another appointment with you?" Cindy asked hopefully.

"I'm done here. There's nothing more I can do; I really deal with those who are possessed or have a demon on the inside. She's clean on the inside. Mostly, she has to start making some smart choices on her own and learn to stand up against the demons."

"How do we help her?" I asked.

"Pray with her, for her, bring her to church, spend time with her."

"But we've been doing that already, and it hasn't exactly stopped her seizures!" I said, my voice escalating. I'd wanted a quick fix or any kind of fix. Hearing that we should continue as we were was not a good enough answer to our problems.

"I know. It takes time. It took her time to get as deeply involved in the occult as she was; it will take time for her to get completely out."

"But surely there's something more that you can do for her?" Cindy asked. She was as agitated as I was.

He looked back and forth between us, seeing our mounting frustration. "Be still and know that I am God. That's from Psalm 46:10. You both need to calm down and let God do the work.

He's capable, you know," he said with twinkling eyes.

I wasn't exactly in a laughing mood, and his attempt to lift us out of our despondency failed miserably. *He might be used to dealing with people like Tammy every day, but I'm not. How can he be so calm about it?*

"She's waking up," he said pointing.

Tammy sat on the pew between us. She apologized, embarrassed for her behavior. Pastor Peterson waved off her apologies with his veined hand and spoke pointedly to her, outlining what she needed to do to get rid of the oppression.

"Get rid of all things occult that you might still own. Stay away from your old friends—anyone who is involved in witchcraft or the occult—don't socialize with them. Tell them about Jesus if you come in contact with them; that will strengthen your own faith. They'll either want nothing to do with you anymore, or they'll stick around to hear more. You also need to speak to the demons frequently, telling them to leave you alone in the name of Jesus. Always use the name of Jesus when you rebuke the demons."

"I can't do that," Tammy said hanging and shaking her head.

"You have to, or they'll never leave you alone. Rhonda and Cindy can do it when they're with you, but the demons will only stay away so long when they do it. It's only when *you* tell them to leave that they'll know you mean business. As a Christian, you have the authority in Jesus Christ to stand against them. Do you understand?"

He was like a kindly grandfather instructing his granddaughter. There was gentleness and kindness in his eyes, but firmness to his voice.

Tammy nodded. Cindy and I looked at each other over her bent head. Neither of us could imagine Tammy being bold enough to stand up to the demons surrounding her; sometimes we felt barely bold enough to do it. The ceiling groaned as though in agony—a reminder of their presence. I visualized the demons sharpening their claws on the roof as they waited impatiently for Tammy to come outside.

"Do you hear them out there?" he asked Tammy. "Most of them stayed outside waiting until you leave, a few of them are right here in the room with us. They'll most likely follow you home. If you want them to leave, you have to tell them so—forcefully. And they *will* leave. They have to in Jesus' name. It may take some time to be rid of them entirely, though, because they'll keep trying to get at you. All three of you need to put on the armor of God every day, and use scripture against them."

He read to us about the armor from Ephesians 6, explaining the different pieces. I'd taken a new interest in the armor since that Sunday standing in front of Tammy's grocery bag full of occult stuff. He gave us a mini sermon on being truthful before God and being righteous and obeying His commandments. "Be ready to tell others about Jesus. Ask God to strengthen your faith so that you can protect yourself against the enemy's arrows. Every day, give your allegiance to Jesus Christ, and trust Him with your salvation. Study the Word and write down verses that you can use against the demons that harass you. Memorize them so that you can use them at any moment, anywhere."

He prayed over the three of us, and especially Tammy, one last time before we were dismissed.

And we were done; the deliverance that never happened was over. We went to all that trouble to find out that Tammy was clean. We brought Tammy there to receive an operation, and it seemed she got a Band-Aid instead. Somehow I expected more. I'd wanted him to fix Tammy as a doctor would remove a diseased appendix. I wanted to hear him say, "You're all better now, just take it easy for a few days then you can get back to normal." Now we were taking Tammy out of there with nothing really changed. We knew more now, but Tammy was still the same.

Somehow Tammy had to be strong enough spiritually to command the demons to quit harassing and oppressing her. It seemed an impossible task. I should have been glad that Tammy wasn't possessed—at least she wasn't still possessed—but getting rid of a few demons inside her seemed easier than dealing with the swarm around her.

Now we had to get Tammy back into my van and then home—through the mob of demons flanking the building. I imagined them with rat-like tails and pointy ears, prominent fangs dripping saliva, long talons ready to dig in and squeeze. We'd suspected for some time that demons were involved with Tammy, but knowing there was a watchful horde outside was not encouraging. They were like thousands of mosquitoes waiting to attack and suck blood. And Tammy was their main prey.

But by this time, we knew that we were also their prey. We had bull's eyes on us just as Tammy did, but for different reasons. She had been in their clutches for years because of her involvement with the occult. We were targeted because we continued to disciple her.

We stood at the double side doors and looked out at a normal parking lot. Just cars and asphalt—nothing more. But we knew they were there now. We'd been told. And none of us were eager to walk through those doors. Obviously we couldn't stay safely in the church forever. We left the building and walked through the unseen horrors around us.

Chapter Ten
HARASSMENT

We were hard pressed on every side, but not crushed; perplexed, but not in despair; persecuted, but not abandoned; struck down, but not destroyed. For our light and momentary troubles are achieving for us an eternal glory that far outweighs them all.
2 Corinthians 4:8, 9, 17

Discipling Tammy had never been easy. We knew that after that Sunday in her apartment, but it became more and more evident as the weeks went by. Tammy was harassed on every side at any given moment, but we also were harassed by demons. At first, we didn't realize what was going on, but one thing mounted upon another until we had a collage of episodes laid before us. After stepping back and acknowledging the number of bad things that happened to us, we finally called them what they were—Satanic attacks.

The attacks started out small. A week after "That Sunday," Keri, Cindy's kindergartner, waited out at the bus stop in vain one Monday morning. Ten minutes, fifteen, twenty past the time it should have been there. But the bus never showed. It was the end of September by then, so this was an oddity since the bus had previously always been there at the end of their driveway to pick Keri up on time. After calling the school, Cindy found out that the bus had indeed arrived there on time. She called the bus company next and they informed her that they didn't have Keri's name on their list.

"But you've been picking her up every day since the beginning of school," Cindy insisted.

"Well, we shouldn't have. She's not on the list," replied the man on the other end.

"But that makes no sense. She must have been on the list before, or the bus never would have stopped to pick her up."

"What's the bus number again?"

"Fifteen."

"That bus doesn't even go down your street."

"Well it has for the last three weeks!" Cindy practically yelled into the phone.

"Look, lady, you'll have to fill out a form in order to get your daughter on the list to get picked up for kindergarten."

"I've already done that," Cindy persisted, trying to control both voice and emotions. She felt like a cat chasing its tail.

"Well, you'll have to do it again!"

"How long will it take before she's picked up again?"

"Three weeks."

"Three weeks! I don't have a car at home. How am I supposed to get my daughter to school for the next three weeks?"

"That's your problem." Cindy heard the phone slam.

She called her neighbor who graciously offered to bring Keri to school that day. Next she called the school and discussed the matter with them. She was worried about sending Keri home on the bus because she wasn't sure if the bus driver was going to stop at their house. She decided to allow her on the bus so long as her teacher, Laura, first checked with the bus driver and explained the situation to him.

Also, the school secretary gave Cindy the number of the man to call at the district office who was in charge of the bus transportation. She made the call and was assured that Keri was on the list and would be picked up from now on. Cindy's worries eased when Keri made it home on the bus just fine that day; the problem seemed to be fixed.

But the next morning the bus was a no-show. It took three days instead of the proposed three weeks to get the situation smoothed out, and once more Keri boarded the bus every morning at the end of her driveway. Cindy was relieved that the predicament was over since her neighbor had to drive Keri to school three days in a row.

Once that was settled, the next harassment dogged its tail. Down in Cindy's basement on the cement floor stood a big, old, cement laundry tub on four narrow legs. But now the tub was cock-eyed because one leg broke through the cement floor. The massive tub had been in the same spot since they'd bought the house and looked as though it had not been moved since the house was built in the '50s. The floor under one leg must have had a hollow pocket in the cement, and the heavy weight of the tub eventually busted through. Cindy was helping Bruce lift the ponderous tub while he shoved a piece of wood under the leg that broke through the floor. She was just wishing that Bruce had asked a man—someone stronger than herself—to help him lift the tub when her grip slipped.

Her fingers scraped along the rough edge of the tub as it slipped out of her grasp and thudded down onto the plank that Bruce had barely managed to slide under the leg in time. Gaping down at her pinky finger—now bent at a right angle to the palm of her right hand, she realized that the floor wasn't the only thing broken now. This wasn't a major medical emergency, but it was painful at the moment and inconveniently taped to the neighboring finger for the next few weeks. Plus, they eventually would have to fix the hole in the floor or else move the heavy tub to a more stable location. They both realized that it could have been worse; at least Bruce hadn't ended up with pancake fingers when Cindy's grip slipped.

Over the course of the few months we ministered to Tammy, we both had electrical difficulties at our houses. Our stereo systems were silenced. We'd been listening to Christian radio and playing Christian records for several weeks, and it must have annoyed Satan and his cohorts. I don't think they preferred praise and worship music. So our stereos quit working.

Practicing what we'd learned from books we'd read recently, we laid hands on them, each in our own home, and prayed forcefully over them, commanding demons out of our stereos in Jesus' name. Even though it felt and sounded a bit ridiculous, it actually worked several times—for Cindy it worked completely. But eventually, my stereo failed to work anymore despite my commands, so I had to take it in for repairs.

It would take three weeks. Three long weeks without my Christian radio station and music was difficult to get through. It seemed lonely during the day without the vibration of music beating through the house. On the appointed day, I went to pick it up, but they couldn't find it. I showed them my receipt. After hunting for what seemed an hour, the guy found it, but it hadn't been looked at yet because it had been tucked away behind some boxes in a corner. Now he told me that it would be three more weeks before it would be ready.

I was frustrated to the point of tears and barely held on to my shattered emotions. Through gritted teeth, I informed them that they'd better get it fixed sooner since I'd already waited three weeks. The man must have had some compassion on my frazzled state because he said he'd see what he could do. It was fixed in two days. Minor frustrations—maybe—but enough to wake us up to the warfare attacks on us.

Satan must not have been getting the results he wanted—leave Tammy alone— because he stepped up the harassment a notch, and then another.

One day I was in the bathroom when Rachel came screaming in, hands waving in the air.

"Mommy, mommy! Come quick! The house is on fire!"

Lord, don't let the house be on fire. Please protect us. I quickly followed Rachel into the kitchen where she stopped to point at the stove with one hand while her other hand tried to stifle the scream rising out of her mouth. Her little legs danced in place on the tile floor. There was indeed a blaze. I turned off the back burner to the gas stove where I had a small pan of eggs boiling gently. Then I turned on the faucet and filled a glass with water and splashed it on the clock on the wall above the stove. I worked hurriedly with a calmness I didn't feel. One more glass of water doused the flames. The plastic sunflower clock was ruined, and the wall behind it was now streaked black.

"How did this happen, Rachel?" I asked, squatting down and grabbing her hands in order to settle her. "Were you in here when it started?"

She nodded and began to cry. "I'm sorry. I'm sorry. I did it!"

"How did you do it? Did you touch the stove?"

"No. I don't know how I did it. I was standing here, and the clock started on fire. I'm sorry. I'm sorry." I hugged her to myself to keep her from getting hysterical.

"If you didn't touch the stove, I'm not sure how you could have done it. Are you sure you didn't turn the knob on the stove?"

"No, no. I didn't touch it, but it's my fault. It started a fire when I was right here." She pointed to the spot on the floor in the middle of the kitchen.

I held her close and calmed her down until she could go back to her toys and play quietly, then I went back into the kitchen to assess the damage and the reason for the fire.

The clock was still on its nail high above the stove, but its cord hung down closer to the stove and it was still plugged in. We'd put up two nails to hold the cord in place so that it wouldn't dangle over the stove. It normally was well out of reach of any flame and there was no way a four-year-old could have reached the cord to take it off its nailed perches. Even off the nails, the cord didn't extend even to the top of the back panel of the stove. *How on earth did it catch fire?*

With the pan of eggs still on the burner, I turned the gas flame back on. Then I flipped it up as high as it would go. The flamed licked around the sides of the pan, but didn't seem to shoot up to where the cord was. I conducted this experiment several times, but each time the flames fell far short of the cord. *And how did the cord get off the nails?*

I had no answer to my inner questions, but I did realize how blessed we were that the whole house hadn't caught fire. I vowed never to leave the stove on without being in the same room with it—even to go to the bathroom! If Rachel had somehow started the fire (which I couldn't understand), I was thankful that she'd warned me so quickly. Darrell was just as stupefied as I'd been about how the fire started, but the clean up wasn't that difficult. The sunflower clock was hopelessly wilted, of course, but the wall cleaned up with a little scraping and a fresh coat of mint green paint.

The fire shook me, though. I slowly began to realize that I was paying a price for ministering to Tammy; the fire could have been a deadly one. Our slight nuisances had turned into near catastrophe, and I wasn't about to take it without a fight. I knew that God had been protecting me and Cindy and our families, but

He did seem to be allowing a certain amount of harassment. My prayers became more targeted at the enemy. Daily I wore my armor and did battle against the evil one, and still he persisted.

About two weeks after the fire incident, Darrell and I took the kids to a movie on a Saturday afternoon. When we arrived home, our house was strangely quiet as Darrell unlocked the door into the entryway. Usually our Sheltie, Mandy, came barking to the door to welcome us home, but now only silence greeted us.

"Something's wrong," I said. "Mandy, come here girl."

No answer.

"Stay here," Darrell said to us. "Let me check out the house."

I stood on the landing just inside the front door with my arms protectively wrapped around all three kids like a mother hen sheltering her chicks. Derek wiggled out from under me, but stood close. It seemed I barely breathed. Darrell climbed the stairs and looked left into the living room, then stepped into the kitchen. He came back and shrugged at the top of the stairs, then moved down the hallway to our bedroom. I couldn't hear anything for what seemed an eternity. Then he came back down the stairs and opened the front door.

"Go outside, all of you and wait by the garage. Our house has been broken into. I'm going to look downstairs."

"Wait!" I anxiously grabbed his sleeve. "Don't go back in there. What if someone's still there?"

Darrell hesitated. "You're right. Let's call the police from the neighbor's house. We all trooped to the gold house one house away from ours; they were friends of ours and had children that played with our girls. They let us in and waited with us until the police came.

"Whoever broke into your house has gone," said the officer after checking it out. "We found your dog huddled up behind a chair in the living room—probably scared to death. We didn't touch her, though. I'm guessing the guy who broke in probably hit her or something. We've had a few burglaries like this recently. He must have been watching the house to see when you all left, then he broke in at your sliding glass door in the basement. The only room that's trashed is the master bedroom. He usually goes straight there and takes only what he can walk away with. You'll have to make a list of the items that are missing."

The officers walked us back to our house. The kids went to find Mandy and cajole her out of her hiding place. She was eager to be picked up and placed on laps and smothered with hugs and petting from the kids.

Darrell and I gazed into our bedroom from its doorway. The floor was littered with our personal items. Tears slipped down my cheek like sap on a maple tree. Every drawer had been removed and its contents spilled on the floor. Nothing remained on top of the dressers, as though someone had swept them clean with a broom. You couldn't take a step into the room without walking on something; every inch of the floor was covered.

I knelt at the doorway and cried.

Then I began there to pick up items to pave a path into the room. T-shirts, bras, panties, sweaters, socks. I felt violated to think that someone went through all my personal items. Old precious pictures dumped out of a box I kept on a shelf in the closet. Some were bent as they'd been strewn about and tramped on. My jewelry box had been overturned onto the bed. Most of what I owned was costume jewelry, but I had a gold cross that seemed to be missing and a sweetheart ring with diamond chips in it from my high school days.

"He usually knows the difference between costume jewelry and the real thing," the officer said.

I mourned my cross. I'd bought it after starting to minister to Tammy, and I usually wore it every day, but that day I'd forgotten to put it on. It had been a precious reminder to me of how close Jesus was to me every moment.

"He took my camera and its case," Darrell announced. He owned a fairly decent camera with various lenses.

"Will he come back?" I asked.

"He usually doesn't, but I'd put a broom handle in your sliding glass door to keep safe until you fix the lock. Actually, I'd keep a broom handle in each of your sliding glass doors for safety. Those are the easiest doors to break into. And make up a detailed list of what was stolen for your insurance and for us. Good-bye now, and I'm sorry this happened to you folks."

Clean-up took all evening. It was a depressing task, knowing that some thief had touched everything. I almost went off the deep end again and washed every item of clothing, but I decided the chore would be too daunting since every drawer had been emptied. We found other items missing, but mostly the absence of my cross and Darrell's camera bothered us. It was difficult to get to sleep and stay asleep that night. Every creak of the house seemed like someone entering to steal from us or harm us. It would be weeks before I slept soundly again.

The fight was on my turf and was getting very personal. Part of me longed for the days when I innocently thought that Satan and his demons wouldn't dare enter my home. Those naïve days seemed a distant memory; I was growing up quickly out of necessity. My spiritual guard was continually up now, and my shield was getting dented with use.

The following Monday, I went over to Cindy's house while Rachel was at preschool. I felt totally drained of energy—a dead battery. "Do you realize how many things have happened to us since we started discipling Tammy?" I asked.

"Yes, I was about to mention that same thing."

We ticked off everything from my nighttime visitation to the break-in.

"We're being attacked, and we need to fight back," I said. "Honestly, I'm getting tired of fighting back."

"I know," Cindy said sympathetically, "And you're getting the worst of it. Satan's trying to get us to stop dealing with Tammy, but we need to continue until God says it's time to stop."

"I agree. I'm just tired of it right now."

We prayed for an hour that day, and God rolled out His thunder and slashed the skies with His lightning. We felt He was backing us up, reviving our strength, our power in His name. The downpour refreshed us as much as it did the earth. We both experienced a hiatus after that—an interval free from attack. I needed the break to strengthen me and prepare me for the worst warfare yet to come.

Satan doubled up both fists and let them fly. It wasn't a direct blow to me, but the strike none-the-less sucked out all my breath and left me gasping for air. He sank to his lowest nature, his evilness bared, his slimy, tricky ways out in the open. He hit my child.

One day after school Derek reached home before Dawn and burst in the door, dumping backpack and jacket at the bottom of the stairs. "Where's your sister?" I asked, since they usually arrived together.

"I don't know. She's slow," he said as he pounded up the stairs and into the kitchen for a snack.

I went downstairs and peaked out the front screen door. There she was meandering down the street into our cul-de-sac, kicking the fresh snow with every step. She twisted and turned, making circled figures in the powder. I began to wonder what was wrong. She was usually my sunshine girl, but now her head hung and her shoulders slumped. I waited by the door to greet her when she arrived from her wandering path.

"Hi honey," I said helping her off with her backpack. "Were you having fun in the snow?"

"I guess. Mom does God ever talk to you?" she asked.

"Well, yes, God talks to me. Why do you ask?"

"I mean out loud, so you can hear him."

"No, He's never talked out loud so I could hear His voice."

She slumped down on the stairway, elbows on knees and chin in her palms.

"You want to talk about something?" I asked sitting on the step beside her.

"Well, is God ever mean?" she asked peering up at me.

"Why don't we go upstairs and talk about this," I said urging her up the stairs with my hand on her back. "God is never mean," I said as we sat together on the couch in the living room. "Why would you ask that question?"

She scrunched up her small face and wound the blond hair from her ponytail around her finger. She shrugged. I waited. "I heard a voice today—at school."

"What did the voice say?" I prompted.

Attempting to mimic the voice, she pursed out her lips and spoke in a low, grating masculine (as well as a nine-year-old girl could muster) voice, "'I'm everywhere, and I'm going to get you and your mom.' Just like that. That's how it sounded, kinda gravelly."

I sucked in my breath and held it. My hand instinctively covered my mouth to keep the gasp inside and safe. Tears sprang to the surface and threatened to well over. I sniffed and blinked, trying to hold back my dangerously whirling emotions from spilling over the edge of the abyss.

"Mommy? Are you okay?"

"Yeah. I'm fine, honey. Um…was that all the voice said?" My voice sounded high and squeaky to my own ears.

"That time, yeah, but later there was more. We were going into the gym for gym class, and we were lined up going through the doorway and it said, 'Look around you.'" Again she mocked the gravelly voice.

"What did that mean?"

"I looked up and all around us, flying over our heads, were these black spidery things." She pumped her slender, out-spread fingers and moved them around in the air above her. "They were about as big as my hands, and they were everywhere—flying all around us. I saw some high up in the corners of the gym. And they were flying above the kids' heads, but some people had more than others. I wanted to swat them away," she said as she flailed her arms and then dropped them dejectedly. "But nobody else seemed to see them, so I pretended that I didn't either. Then he laughed, 'Heh, heh, heh.' He sounded so mean, like he was laughing at me cause I was scared."

I lost the battle for control, and tears slid down my cheeks; Dawn followed suit. We held onto each other—tightly. I rubbed her back. My little girl was looking to me to fix things, to solve her problems, and I was seemingly causing them. I immediately discerned that the voice did not belong to God, but instead to Satan or a demon. The black spider-like things she saw buzzing around were probably demons. I knew they existed in the spiritual world, but Dawn being able to see them seemed like something out of a horror movie. This was a demonic attack upon my daughter! I was both angry and hurt. *Why would you allow this, Lord? I'm doing what You asked me to do. You got me involved with Tammy. You started this whole mess, now You have to fix things. You have to protect her. She's only nine!*

My prayer didn't waft into nothingness, but shot straight as an arrow to the heart of God. As I sat holding Dawn, He stilled my knotting insides then injected me with enough adrenaline to fight the enemy—again. I knew who to direct my anger and energy against. *He's gone too far this time!*

"Dawn, that wasn't God you heard today. God is never mean. He would never scare you or laugh at you. He loves you and wants to protect you from the devil. You know mommy is teaching Tammy lots of stuff about Jesus, right?" She nodded. "Well, Tammy was involved in some pretty bad stuff—things God doesn't want us to do, and now she's a Christian. But the enemy, the devil, is angry at her for not liking him anymore, and he's trying to get back at her. The devil is mad at me too, because I'm trying to help Tammy. Do you understand?"

She nodded again. My explanation seemed to be sinking in and making sense. "That's why some bad things have been happening around here—like the fire in the kitchen and the burglary. Well, those things didn't stop me from working with Tammy so the devil is trying harder. I believe it was the devil or maybe a demon who spoke to you today. And it was probably demons that you saw flying around in the gym. For some reason God allowed it, but he wants to protect you, so we have to fight back. Mommy prays all the time against the devil, telling him to go away and leave me alone. I'm going to teach you how to do that too. Okay? You can be a soldier for God—just like Mommy!"

The excitement in my voice infected her, and she eagerly bobbed her head. "Can I wear a cross like you?" I fingered the new gold cross and chain I'd immediately bought after the break-in.

"We'll see about getting you a cross necklace, but until then we can make a cross to tape to your desktop at school. And we can make it as big as you like and put Bible verses on it. That way, if the devil ever talks to you again, you can look at your cross and say the verses that we write on it. Does that sound like a good plan?"

"Yeah! I'm gonna go down and get my markers and paper. Can we do it on the kitchen table?"

"Yes, that's a good place. That way you can work on it while I'm fixing supper. And I can help you when you need it."

She ran downstairs, rummaged around in her stash of art supplies and came tromping back up the stairs and dumped everything on the kitchen table. She had markers, paper, scissors and glue.

She chose a pure white piece of construction paper. She began drawing a large, wide cross on it big enough to fill the page top to bottom, side to side. Outlining the cross in purple, her favorite color, she next put colorful "gems" on the cross. Then she drew a circle in red on top of the cross but as though it were behind the cross, connecting its arms.

While she was drawing, I looked up passages in my Bible and wrote a few down. "Are you ready to hear some Bible passages?" I asked her when she completed her cross. I read several to her, and she chose some. We also decided that she would write down words that she could speak out loud to the devil when he bothered her.

On the crossbeam of her cross, she wrote in big bold letters: "Jesus loves me. I am a child of God" (from 1 John 3:1). Vertically, she wrote: "I love Jesus." "Get away from me, Satan" from Matthew 4:10 stood in prominence atop the cross. Bending on the top two arcs of her circle she copied scripture. James 4:7: "Resist the devil and he will flee from you" and 1 Peter 5:9: "Resist him, standing firm in the faith." Underneath each arc she wrote: "I resist you in Jesus' name." Taking out her blue marker, she placed more scripture outside the two bottom arcs: "I am sprinkled by Christ's blood" (from 1 Peter 1:2) and "They overcame him by the blood of the Lamb" (Revelation 12:11). She drew drops of blood coming down on a picture of herself and flowing from the side of a lamb.

In the two bottom quadrants, she marked: "The Lord will keep you from all harm—he will watch over your life" (Psalm 121:7) and "But the Lord is faithful, and he will strengthen and protect you from the evil one." She drew little pictures in the open spaces, and when she finished, the end result was a masterpiece of color, design and neatness.

"Dawn, it's beautiful! Wait till Daddy gets home; he's going to love it. Why don't you leave it here on the table so he can see it, then you can clean up your stuff and go play for awhile."

After she when downstairs, I called the school and asked for Laura. When she answered, I told her the whole story of the voice and told her about the cross Dawn had made.

"Rhonda, if Dawn needs me any time at school, she can come down to my room, and I'll pray with her."

Tears spilled afresh, "Is that okay? I mean can she do that? Will her teacher let her?"

"I'll explain the situation to her teacher, and I'm sure she'll understand."

"She's going to think we're all crazy!"

"Don't worry about it; I'll take care of it. If Dawn hears the voice again and needs my help, she should just tell her teacher she needs to see me and then come down to my room. I'll drop everything and pray with her. The kids can keep busy for a few moments without me."

"Thank you. That means a lot to me," I choked out. Now that Dawn wasn't in the room, I was slowly coming unglued.

"Don't worry about it. I'll help any way I can; you know that. I'll pray for you guys as soon as we hang up, okay?"

"Okay, bye."

Next I called Cindy and explained the whole thing to her. She sympathized and prayed with me over the phone, beating the devil verbally with a stick.

It looked as though we'd be having leftovers that night; I hadn't managed the time nor the energy to get anything started. I couldn't even think of possibilities. When Darrell came home, I explained everything to him and showed him Dawn's cross.

"Maybe it's time you stopped discipling Tammy," he said as he held me.

I backed off. It's not as though I hadn't thought of it during the last several weeks and especially that afternoon, but I knew I couldn't drop Tammy.

"God got me into this; He'll have to get me out of it," I said. "Somehow I think I'll know when I'm done with Tammy—God will release me."

"But, Rhonda, this is our daughter we're talking about! Don't you think enough is enough?"

I understood his reasoning; it made more earthly sense to stop ministering to Tammy, but it wasn't spiritually right. "If I quit now, Satan wins," I said tiredly. I didn't need to battle Darrell, too; I had my hands full with the devil. "I can't let him win. It's just not right. We need to trust God that he will protect her—and us. We need to pray more, use the authority over demons that Jesus gave us. I just can't quit; you have to understand that!"

I was wandering close to the brink and needed his support desperately. Taking me into his arms again, he sighed, "All right, we'll do it together. We'll battle him together."

The next day after school, I waited impatiently pacing in front of the window until the bus drove by. As Dawn came up the driveway, I could see the tears streaking her cheeks and she was holding something in her hand.

"Mommy, somebody tore it up!" she cried as she threw herself against me. Out of her hand she dropped a dozen pieces of white construction paper that used to be her cross. "I put it on my desk, but after recess, I came back and it was torn. I taped it up, but after lunch it was ripped up like this." She cried like a little girl who'd lost her best friend.

"We'll make another one just like the first one. Did you hear the voice today?"

"No," she sobbed. At least she hadn't had to deal with that.

I found a sturdier piece of paper--poster board--and she went to work with her markers, designing the cross in the same manner as before. Her little heart wasn't nearly as joyful in the project as the day before.

At 4:00 the next afternoon, I looked at the same tear-streaked face of the day before. "What happened this time?"

She dumped the pieces into my cupped palms. Her chin jutted out stubbornly. "I'm going to make another one and tape it down so much to my desk that no one can rip it up!

"That's my girl! We'll beat Satan this time, won't we? Did you tell your teacher?"

"Yes. She said if I make another one, she's going to tell everybody they'll be in big trouble if they touch my cross!" She muttered to herself as she stomped down the stairs to get more supplies.

I found some clear packaging tape and handed it to her. "Ask your teacher before you use this; she may not want you to. But if she allows it, this may solve the problem.

The tape and her teacher's warning did the trick, and the cross remained on Dawn's desktop from the end of November through January—until she no longer needed it. She had a few more instances where she heard the same gravelly voice again and even saw the spidery demons. Laura faithfully prayed with Dawn anytime she needed her.

Just as Dawn had seen the demons at school, one day she also saw them at home. She came running upstairs shouting that they were downstairs flying around. As I hugged her, she said, "Oh, mommy, they're in your kitchen too!"

"How many do you see?" I asked.

"Only two. But there's more downstairs. Come look."

"Honey, I'm afraid I can't see them. Let's call Cindy and see if she can come over and help me pray them out of the house, okay?"

Cindy was able to drop everything and come over. We took the cross down from the wall and prayed over every room just as we had when Ray came over. It didn't take as long this time, but we chased every spidery demon out of the house. Dawn kept us informed on where they were and when they were all gone.

Two occurrences where she heard the voice happened in December. When the classroom Christmas tree went up, Dawn stood alone in front of it admiring the twinkling white lights. The voice said, "Put your hand under the lights." Dawn complied, and her hand turned a myriad of colors as though the lights were rainbows. "I can do other magical tricks for you." Dawn ran to tell her teacher and was given permission to go down the hall to Laura's room for prayer.

Also in December, Cindy and I spoke about our experience with Tammy at the local Christian high school located just across the street from Dawn's school. At the precise moment that Cindy and I exited my car and were walking up to the front doors of the school, Dawn heard the voice. "Go over to the windows." Again, Dawn did so without thinking, obedient as a puppy learning new tricks. "See your mom? She thinks she's pretty tough, but I'm going to get her." Dawn ran down the hallway to Laura's room, hysterically crying. She was so afraid that Satan would "get me." Laura prayed with her and was able to calm her down enough for her to return to her classroom. That was the last time she heard the voice.

Although attacking my daughter was the worst harassment I had to suffer, Satan did indeed try to "get me." Cindy and I had spoken about our experience a few times and we'd made tapes of two of our engagements. Since people were asking for tapes, we decided to make a composite to hand out to those who wanted one. As I was on my way down to a college that had the equipment we needed to produce the tapes, an accident occurred.

The car in front of me and in the right lane beside me was struck forcefully on the right by a fast, oncoming truck from the perpendicular street. He impacted the car's passenger door with his front end. I didn't have time to stop and braced myself for the full collision of both cars slamming into me as I went into the intersection, but there was no impact. I opened my eyes to see the truck stopped dead and the car had miraculously swerved back into its own lane. I slowly drove by the mangled vehicles, praying.

After pulling over to the side of the road to catch my breath and glue together my fractured nerves, I had a strong sense that the truck was meant for me. Even though I didn't receive the full weight of the truck smashing into me, I was amazed that I'd sailed through the intersection unscathed. I didn't understand how they'd both stopped in time and how the car hadn't fishtailed into my lane. It seemed physically impossible. I said a "thank you" prayer before starting on my way again.

Some of the attacks were small inconveniences, some were trying experiences, some were near major mishaps and one was a challenge that nearly tore me apart, but all were doomed to failure. Satan did not get his desired effect because I still continued to minister to Tammy.

Each harassment made a dent in my armor, but I stood strong. Each arrow, each dart, each club delivered hard blows that shook me, staggered me, but didn't mow me down. God was faithful despite the harassment. And he built a stronger me. I now knew how to confront the enemy, to take up my shield and sword and to fight back. I wore the authority of Jesus as a mantle, covering my head, protecting and strengthening my spirit. My goal was to hear Jesus say, "Well done, my good and faithful servant."

Chapter Eleven
RENOUNCING

He who conceals his sins does not prosper, but whoever confesses and renounces them finds mercy.
Proverbs 28:13

"Tammy has asked me to baptize her, and she wants you and Cindy to be there," Pastor Ken said. "Since she's in the hospital so often, I think it would be wise to just baptize her in the hospital."

"When were you planning on doing it?" I asked, moving over towards the kitchen sink and away from my family's noise at the table. I knew that Tammy had expressed an interest in being baptized and so Pastor Ken had been teaching her about it. I wasn't even surprised by his suggestion that we do it in the hospital; it seemed safer really, since she continually had seizures.

"I know this is short notice, but tomorrow after church would work for me—about 2:00? Do you think you can make it?"

"Sure, I'll be there. I can call Cindy for you. I'll call back only if there's a problem; otherwise, we'll meet you at the hospital at two."

It had been several weeks since Tammy had met with Pastor

Peterson. As suspected, she was having trouble using her authority in Christ to command the demons away from her. But she was working on it. The problem was getting them before they got her. Most of the time, she was like a marionette on strings jerked by the demons, having seizures at their will. She'd had so many seizures that she was black and blue from falling down and banging around. Her doctors didn't know what else to do but place her in the hospital and monitor her. Not that it helped any; she still continued to seizure daily. However, when we were with her, the demons began leaving her alone. I'm sure they hung around just waiting to pounce on her and torment her further, creating as much havoc with her as possible.

Pastor Peterson had been right about the mob of demons following her everywhere. In the last few weeks, Tammy had been attacked twice on the streets of her neighborhood. Once, she was walking home from the corner store with her bag full of groceries, and a man ran by her, bumped her, grabbed the bag right out of her arms and took off down the street before she had a chance to scream.

The other time, she was out walking near her apartment, and a man she'd never seen before approached her. He snarled in her face saying, "I know who you are. You're a witch pretending to be a Christian. You'll never make it. We'll never let you go." Then he proceeded to smack her and punch her, and when she fell to the ground, he kicked her. This episode landed her in the hospital again with more bruises. She was beginning to look like a rainbow with her bruises at different stages of healing, but she felt like Satan's punching bag. Evil dogged her every move like a wolf following its prey.

Clearly, Tammy was making headway though. She was able to read her Bible without it being hot. Jan had quit calling and hounding her. Her former witch friends left her alone after making a final in-your-face appeal to Tammy. Between the six of us—the older couple, Pastor Ken and Nancy, and Cindy and I— she kept us fairly busy praying, teaching, chauffeuring, visiting and generally helping her make it through every day. We were her dependable tag team at her beck and call. We were thrilled with her progress and growth; every baby step forward made her spiritually stronger and loosened Satan's grasp on her. And now Tammy was ready to be baptized.

Cindy was able to attend the baptism, so I drove the two of us to the hospital on Sunday afternoon. Although Pastor Ken still had his suit and clerical collar on, we dressed comfortably in jeans and sweaters. We never knew how much floor time would be required of us, so we always tried to be comfortable.

While we waited, we looked around the lounge. "Oh my gosh, Cindy look at this," I hissed in a stage whisper, grabbing her arm and turning her in the direction I was gaping.

Posted on a whiteboard set up on a tripod was an announcement for Friday evening's video choices. The patients voted by placing hash marks next to the video they'd prefer viewing. *Bambi* lost with a measly two votes; it looked like the residents of the psychiatric ward would be viewing *Halloween* tomorrow night.

"I can't believe it," Cindy said, stunned.

"Are they nuts? Who in their right mind would show a horror flick to psych patients?" I asked. I was outraged and dumbfounded at the same time. There seemed no end to the surprises surrounding Tammy.

Tammy had told us about her hospital stay. On the first day, a male nurse came to her room, and before he left he told her he would come back tomorrow. Tammy said she asked him not to, but as promised, he showed up with the board the next day and took it out of the box without even asking her. She said he ignored her protests at first, but she finally managed to convince him that she didn't want to play.

Witches in social services, horror movies shown in psych wards, nurses with Ouija Boards. What next?

When we entered her room, Tammy was in high spirits.. She greeted us enthusiastically with big hugs. This seemed a banner day for her, a day of choice.

Pastor Ken got right down to business, and it looked as though this would be a formal affair even though it was in a hospital room. We gathered in a circle, Pastor with the hymnal and his Bible open underneath it. He began with a lengthy prayer and then read some scripture about baptism. So far Tammy was holding up nicely. She was as serious about this as a person could be with a grin swiping across her face.

Pastor asked us all to recite the Lord's Prayer together, which Tammy knew because she'd been working on memorizing it. Then he gave her a charge to read the scriptures, attend church services and instruction in the Christian faith, and to lead a godly life until Jesus Christ returned.

"Do you renounce the devil and all his works and all his ways."

"Yes," Tammy replied.

"Tammy, I feel strongly that you need to confess and renounce your involvement in the occult," Pastor Ken said.

Tammy looked at each of us. We nodded encouragement. Cindy and I had talked with Pastor Ken about this some time ago. From all the books we'd read about the occult and getting out of its bondage, renouncing all her participation in witchcraft seemed the right thing to do and the proper next step. As we'd learned about different occult practices, Cindy and I had realized there were bones buried in our own childhoods. Tammy had uncovered many practices for us. As she revealed her involvement in séances, horoscopes, playing the Ouija Board and other habits, we'd both had to look into the mirrors of our own pasts and found some of the same entanglements with the occult. Although our participation had been minor compared to hers, we had done some renouncing of our own. Now it was Tammy's turn.

"I need to kneel for this," she said. And we all decided to kneel on the tile floor beside her.

"I don't even know where to begin," she said.

"Take your time," Pastor Ken said. Little did he realize what he was saying.

Tammy took him at his word, and for the next hour, she confessed every possible occult involvement she could think of. We moved from knees to bottoms after fifteen minutes; when the cold of the tile seeped through our jeans, we stood. Pastor sat in a chair and pulled it up close to keep a tight circle around Tammy. But Tammy remained faithfully on her knees the whole time, head bent and confessing.

"I'm going to try to start at the beginning," she said. "I renounce all the occult practices that I was involved in with my mom."

"Tammy, can you name each thing separately rather than lumping them together?" Pastor Ken suggested.

"Okay. I renounce séances, consulting the dead, gazing at crystal balls, levitation, playing the Ouija Board, tarot cards, trances, palm reading, horoscopes," she recited the list slowly. "I think that's all I did at home with my mom and her friends. They'd do different things on different days; it was never the same."

I recognized most of her list, in fact I was guilty of some of it myself. Cindy and I had renounced the Ouija Board and things we'd done at slumber parties like mock séances, but instead of crystal balls, we'd used the 8-ball (A black ball with a window for answers on the bottom; it's still sold in stores today). But one thing neither of us recognized. "What are tarot cards Tammy?" I asked.

"It's a deck of cards with pictures on them; each card stands for something. They're used to tell fortunes. A lot of what my mom and her friends did was to tell fortunes or find out the future. They used tarot cards all the time."

"I didn't mean to interrupt; I just wanted to understand all that you're renouncing."

"I think it's a good idea to ask questions, but perhaps we should save that until the end, so long as it's okay with you, Tammy?" Pastor Ken asked.

"Sure. I'm ready to go on now." We nodded. "Lord, I confess that I hated my dad, my mom and even my brother and sister. I confess that I wanted my dad dead, and I thought of ways that I could kill him. I even tried casting spells on him when I was a teenager, but none of it worked." She started crying, her shoulders shaking.

We put our arms around her and Cindy said, "It's okay, Tammy. It's good to get it out and give it to Jesus."

When Tammy collected herself, she continued, "Next, I guess I met Jan and got involved in more stuff with her. I renounce my involvement in witchcraft. I renounce casting spells, meditation, visiting Jan's coven, the rituals we did, wearing crystals, charming and magic—both white and black magic, bewitching, channeling, table tapping, calling up demons, worshiping Satan, making an oath to Satan and writing my name in his book in blood, drinking blood, practicing ESP, astral projection." Again she recited her list slowly as she thought of more items to add to it. "That's all I can think of."

Cindy and I raised our eyebrows at each other. We were still learning the depth of witchcraft. It seemed like an endless list of things you could involve yourself in once you started on the path downward into the abyss. I made a mental note to ask Tammy about some of the things she mentioned on her list that I'd never heard of before.

"Perhaps you should continue, Tammy," Pastor Ken suggested, looking at his watch.

Tammy bent her head again, "Okay. Jesus, I renounce my school lessons with Wicca, teaching me how to do horoscopes, cast spells, divination, all about witchcraft rituals and worshiping Satan and goddesses. I renounce all the objects that they sent me in the mail—the crystals and jewelry, the candles and candleholders, the skull, the Ouija Board. I renounce the objects I had in my apartment like the owls and unicorn."

There was silence for a while, and we patiently waited.

Pastor opened his Bible to Exodus 20. "Tammy, I'm going to read the Ten Commandments from the Bible. I'll stop after each one to give you time to think. Maybe this will prompt your memory a bit."

"All right," she nodded.

"'You shall have no other gods before me.'"

"Lord, I've had other gods—Satan and goddesses that I've worshiped."

"'You shall not make for yourself an idol in the form of anything in heaven above or on the earth beneath or in the waters below. You shall not bow down to them or worship them; for I, the Lord your God, am a jealous God, punishing the children for the sin of the fathers to the third and fourth generation of those who hate me, but showing love to a thousand generations of those who love me and keep my commandments.'"

"God, forgive me for using other things as idols, worshiping them and looking to them to help me instead of You."

"'You shall not misuse the name of the Lord your God, for the Lord will not hold anyone guiltless who misuses his name.'"

"Lord, so many times I've used your name as a swear word; I've made fun of You and Your name. Please forgive me." She recounted times when she was with Jan and other witches when they scoffed at the Christian God.

"'Honor your father and your mother, so that you may live long in the land the Lord your God is giving you.'"

Tammy lifted her head and looked over at us as if to say, *Not again*. "I think we've covered that one several times over," I said. "You can go on to the next one."

"'You shall not murder.'"

Tammy sucked in her breath, covered her face with her hands and started weeping. We all looked at each other, bracing ourselves for the worst. Visions of human sacrifices swept through my mind like an eerie nightmare. I'd read too many books stating that human sacrifices, though rare, continued today. But none of us wanted to voice our fears that Tammy had killed someone. We simply kept our arms around her until she could talk.

"I've had two abortions," she choked out between sobs. "One when I was 18, and the other when I was 21. Jan helped me get them." Tammy began rocking back and forth on her knees and holding her stomach.

I sat back on my heels as though someone had punched me. Even though abortions were legal, I'd known in my heart that an abortion was the murder of a baby. I'd never known anyone who'd had an abortion, and momentarily, I was speechless. But the silence after her admission seemed to hang in the air like a glass teetering on the edge waiting to shatter. I had to say something.

"Tammy, abortion is serious. I believe it is murder." I paused, wondering how to continue. *Help me out, Lord.* "So, you would have had two children that are now dead because you aborted them. Tammy, I believe you will be able to see those children in heaven when you get there."

"That's right, Tammy," Cindy added. "I think God has your babies with him now in heaven."

"But God forgives all sins when we confess them to Him," I said. "God will forgive any sin. Sometimes we think one sin is worse than another, but God looks at all sin the same. It's wrong, and He wants us to confess it."

Tammy looked up at Pastor Ken for confirmation. He nodded in agreement. "Go ahead, Tammy, and confess your sin."

"God, forgive me for killing my babies." And she broke down again into spasms of crying. Pastor Ken walked over to the bedside cart and brought the Kleenex box over and laid it in front of Tammy. She honked, dabbed and sniffled until she was able to compose herself again.

"Should we go on, Tammy?" Pastor asked. Tammy's head bobbed. "'You shall not commit adultery.'"

"Did I commit adultery?" she asked.

"Were you married to the men who fathered your children?" he asked.

"No. Jesus, forgive me for my adultery with ..." and she named four different males.

"'You shall not steal.'"

"I only remember stealing small stuff as a kid." She added her confession.

"'You shall not give false testimony against your neighbor.'"

She confessed some lies she'd told about people.

"'You shall not covet your neighbor's house. You shall not covet your neighbor's wife, or his manservant or maidservant, his ox or donkey, or anything that belongs to your neighbor.'"

She didn't have much to confess after that one—most of it dealt with her brother and sister. She had definitely wanted the status, care and things that were given to them but not to her.

"Tammy, is there anything else you want to confess before I baptize you?"

Tammy bent her head. "I confess that I've been drunk before and tried some drugs."

Pastor Ken said, "Upon this your confession, I, by virtue of my office, as a called and ordained servant of the Word, announce the grace of God unto you, and in the stead and by the command of my Lord Jesus Christ I forgive you all your sins in the name of the Father and of the Son and of the Holy Spirit. Amen."

"Now we can get on with the baptism," he said. And he proceeded to baptize her right there in her hospital room with water from her little bathroom. "I baptize you in the name of the Father, and of the Son, and of the Holy Spirit. Amen."

Tammy wiped herself dry, and beamed at us through watery, red-rimmed eyes. We all took turns hugging her.

Pastor Ken prepared to leave, but Cindy and I wanted to stick around a little longer to ask Tammy about some of those items she renounced. We said our good-byes to him, then asked Tammy if we could ask her a few questions. She agreed, even though she looked a bit tired by now. She climbed into the bed and sat with the covers tucked under her armpits.

"I've heard you mention most of that stuff before," I said, "but there's a few things on your list I didn't recognize—what's the difference between white and black magic?"

"Well, white magic doesn't hurt anyone; it's supposed to be used to help you or someone else. Like doing a spell to help someone get a job or for healing someone who's sick. They start you out with white magic, then later on they teach you black magic. That would be casting spells against someone you hate or using evil spirits to gain power over someone. Jan and her coven did stuff like that; I hadn't done too much black magic yet."

"What is channeling?" Cindy asked.

"Channeling is sort of like meditation. You empty your mind and invite spirits to take control of your mind and body and speak through you. The spirits that you channel are supposed to help you."

"And what exactly do you mean by charming?" I asked.

"Do you guys remember that I had some crystals?" Cindy and I nodded. "Those are used for charming. They're supposed to contain positive energy and be good luck for you. There are other things that can be used as charms; usually people wear them around their necks. Sometimes they're called amulets. Charming just means depending on these things for good luck, to keep you safe—that kind of thing."

"One more thing," I added. "What is bewitching?"

"That's casting a spell over someone or something, sort of making them come under your power." She hesitated. "My bird was bewitched."

"By the way, what ever happened to your bird, Tammy?" Cindy asked.

"I gave it back to Debbie and Cheryl."

"I guess I have another question," Cindy said. "I don't know what astral projection is—could you explain it?"

"Well, some witches can do it, but it seems like only those who are deep into witchcraft are able to. You're supposed to meditate and get yourself into a trance, and then at some point you can have an out of body experience where you actually leave your earthly body and travel to other places."

She looked at us tiredly, "Are you guys done? I'm kind of tired now."

"We're sorry, Tammy," Cindy said. "Thank you for answering our questions, though. I think we've asked you enough for now."

We each gave her another hug and prayed a short prayer over

her before we left. We'd been there over two hours. Nothing was ever fast when we dealt with Tammy; it seemed as though everything took hours longer than we thought it would. The amazing part about the afternoon was that Tammy didn't have even one seizure. We wondered aloud why the mob of demons left her alone during this time so that she could finish her confessing and renouncing and continue with her baptism. Maybe God had held back the throng during the afternoon just like He'd held back the Red Sea for the children of Israel.

I hope the horde of demons drown like the Egyptians when God allows the sea to return to normal, I thought as we said our good-byes.

Cindy and I decided to stop for fast food on the way home. As usual after spending time with Tammy, we were starving. It seemed that we always expended our fuel reserves when we were with her.

"I know we've done some renouncing ourselves before this," I said, "but when Tammy was confessing, there were several of the things she mentioned that I've done myself. I just forgot about them."

"I know," Cindy said. "I still can't believe I participated in mock séances. Nothing ever happened, but we did that several times when I was growing up."

"Yeah, we held séances where nothing happened except that we got scared. But we did levitation where we gathered around someone lying on the floor, and each of us would place two fingers underneath her. Then we'd each chant something, lifting her up with only our fingers. That always worked, but I don't remember what we chanted."

"Something about being light as a feather; we did it too."

"I'd forgotten about that until Tammy mentioned it. I also forgot about the palm reading. My high school had a palm reader at our post prom party. Also, I had my palm read at the fair once," I said.

"I wonder if there's anything else we've forgotten," Cindy mused.

We both chewed silently for a while. "I think when I go home, I'm going to get on my knees and renounce these things and ask God if there's anything else buried in my past," I said.

"Me too," Cindy added. "Another thing. I think I'm going to make a thorough search of my house and get rid of anything that might have occult ties. As Tammy was confessing worshiping other gods, God reminded me that my uncle gave me a gold charm of a Buddha for my charm bracelet when I was in high school. I never attached it to my bracelet, but I might still have it somewhere. I bet there's other stuff that needs to be thrown out."

"You're right. I think we should pray in our own homes and ask God to show us what needs to be tossed. I threw away that macramé owl right after Tammy told me about their use of owls, but I bet there's other stuff to toss out now that I know more. I'll start tomorrow."

The next morning, Cindy and I both started the process of determining what could stay and what had to go. We each roamed our houses praying and looking for things that might have occult ties or might be displeasing to God. It took us well over two weeks before we declared our homes "clean." We prayed, sorted, studied, prayed some more.

Cindy and I both threw out a few books that were of questionable content. Music was a venue that took a major cut in both of our households. Darrell owned almost all the albums we had from before our marriage. I was never into rock music much and didn't spend my money on albums, but Darrell had three to four dozen. I scrutinized each one, ending up with a sizable pile to toss—but not without his consent. I felt he had to okay throwing them out.

Some album covers were clearly occult in nature because of the symbols used on the cover. I didn't want to own albums that sported a pentagram or goat's head on the cover. The ankh, yin-yang and broken crosses (like the swastika and the peace symbol) or crosses in circles were other symbols I didn't want in my house. I'd read *Mystery Mark of the New Age* (Crossway Books) by Texe Marrs, and it had opened my eyes to the uses of many symbols in New Age worship.

If I was unsure about an album, I read the words to the songs. I didn't want lyrics espousing drug use or occult worship. Later, Darrell took a look at the questionable albums with me and he agreed to pitch the whole pile. It greatly depleted our store of music, but we'd since switched over to listening to Christian music most of the time anyway, so it was no great loss to either of us. Cindy and Bruce had a similar pile at their home that ended up in the trash.

Next, I went to the basement and looked over my children's toys, games and books. Tucked away in Derek's closet, I found an unopened box. His grandmother had given him a Dungeons and Dragons game for his birthday, but it had remained on the shelf of his closet sealed shut for over a year. She bought the game because a store clerk told her it was the latest rave in games for kids. We were game players at our house, so it amazed me that we'd never opened it. Now I thanked God that we'd never played it. A dragon symbol on almost anything spells trouble since the dragon is the symbol for Satan. I'd also read a book about the game and how dangerous it was to become hooked on it. That immediately became garbage.

Looking through my children's toys and deciding what to throw out became the toughest choices of all. Again I had read about children's toys and Saturday morning cartoons. Some articles condemned practically every cartoon and all the toys that went along with them. I felt discernment was in order. I watched the cartoons with my children the next Saturday.

I tried to judge between witchcraft or New Age and simple make believe. After all, the fairy tales that we all know and love contain some make believe and many contain witches. Should I build a wall around my children, never allowing them to see anything that might be considered at all questionable? Or do I teach my children to discriminate between true evil and make believe?

I drew the line when I saw true witchcraft portrayed as fun and harmless. I drew the line when make believe turned over-the-edge evil. Some shows became off-limits to my children's viewing, and we had good discussions about my reasons why. Since they had followed along closely with what went on with Tammy, they didn't object to my nixing certain shows. Selected toys also were tossed, but never without the okay of my child. A similar process was taking place at Cindy's, and we both agreed on which toys and shows to ban.

Our house cleaning went beyond physical evidence of the occult; it went to our hearts. If our children weren't allowed to watch particular shows, Darrell and I had to clean up our acts also. Not allowing questionable lyrics to penetrate our ears was a first step, but we also made new choices on what our eyes took in. Some TV shows and movies now were on our banned list. I became very sensitive to shows and movies that portrayed witchcraft. I'd seen what involvement in it had done to one person, and I could no longer stand to watch it on the screen. Whether it was shown as pure evil to be wiped out and overcome or depicted as fun, cute and harmless didn't matter to me. I hated both pictures.

Another practice that involved our whole family and brought us together for a serious discussion was Halloween. Previously we'd allowed our children to "trick or treat" every Halloween, but I always hated the practice. Now I knew why. Research shined a light on Halloween.

Halloween is the premier holy day for witches; it is called Samhain in honor of the lord of the dead. It is also known as the "festival of the dead." All the practices associated with Halloween are steeped in occultism and Satanism from the wearing of costumes to begging for candy.

On the Halloween right after I met Tammy, my children dressed up as usual and went out trick or treating, but I stayed home to hand out candy to those who came to the door. My stomach churned as I saw child after child dressed as devils, witches, mass murderers, gory masks dripping fake blood. Not all were dressed this way, but most groups of children contained at least one objectionable costume. Everywhere I looked, society seemed caught up in the grisly celebration—skeletons, black spiders, ugly witches, gruesome masks, headless straw-stuffed bodies lounging in front of stores or houses. My sensitivities to the evil and hideousness spiked that October, and I decided I couldn't do Halloween anymore.

After Tammy's renouncing, our family talked about Halloween and what to do on that day. We decided that we'd find other alternatives rather than celebrate that day the same way we'd always done it. Every one of my children agreed to other activities on that night next year, and I supplied the candy that they would miss.

Cindy's family went through the same discussion about Halloween that we had. She was particularly mortified at the remembrance of her daughter Keri's costume when she was four years old—just the year before. Cindy had dressed her up as a witch, complete with black dress, pointy hat and even a large wart on her face. This year it wasn't funny, though. It really tore at her heart to think that she'd dressed Keri up that way, so she repented before the Lord and vowed never to do that again. In the following years, our families often got together for wholesome fun activities rather than "trick or treating."

Tammy's renouncing set off a flood of decisions for both Cindy and I and our families. While we were busy cleaning house—inside and out, Tammy suffered a higher level of demonic attack than before.

The night of Tammy's renouncing and baptism, the nurses recorded 27 seizures. In the following week, Tammy endured more seizures than they could count. She remained hospitalized for well over a week before they felt she was well enough and stabilized enough to go home.

Returning home was difficult for Tammy and for us. She needed so much attention, and when she didn't get it, she manufactured reasons for us to "help" her. The strain of ministering to her on a daily basis was taking its toll on all of us, and we agreed that Tammy needed more help than we could collectively offer her. Someone told us about Teen Challenge.

Although Teen Challenge is mainly for young people who have been involved in drug and alcohol abuse, we called and found out that they occasionally took people who had been involved in the occult. Their day-to-day, on-site care complete with spiritual help in overcoming whatever they were in bondage to seemed just what Tammy needed. She had an interview with the people from Teen Challenge and they agreed to take her—but only if she went to another state's facility instead of the one in Minneapolis. They wanted to remove her from her environment and give her new roots.

Tammy agreed to enter their program, and she left at the end of January, 1985, without us knowing where they were taking her. We hoped to see her again, but that was up to Tammy after she graduated from Teen Challenge.

Tammy's departure left a void in our lives. We barely knew what "normal" was anymore. We felt strongly that God had released us from our ministry to Tammy, but there was also a sense of loss. So much of our days surrounded her needs that without her, we seemed lost—almost like an empty-nest syndrome. What we didn't miss was the harassment; it seemed to ebb but not entirely disappear with Tammy's separation from us.

Slowly we returned to a new level of normal. Our Bible studies receded to a manageable level, but God continued to feed us through His word. Cindy and I continued to meet together to pray. Bruce expressed a desire to pray with us, then another couple from our church began meeting with us and shortly after that, my own husband decided to join us. We formed a core small group that eventually grew to five couples. Though some of the faces are different now, most remain the same, and our small group continues to meet today to pray and share testimonies of what God is still doing in our lives.

Chapter Twelve

LESSONS LEARNED

Finally, brothers, whatever is true, whatever is noble, whatever is right, whatever is pure, whatever is lovely, whatever is admirable-- if anything is excellent or praiseworthy--think about such things.
Philippians 4:8

Like waves rippling outward from a stone dropped in water, so was the effect of Tammy on our lives. Tammy was the initial beneficiary of my witnessing to her, but I benefited spiritually also. I spread outward when I involved Cindy, and we both rippled towards our husbands, friends and families. When the Holy Spirit filled us, we overflowed our shores and wet anyone who would listen. I believe the sanctifying work of the Holy Spirit is to be shared with others just as the redeeming work of Jesus in our lives is to be our testimony. It's impossible to keep something so good, so wonderful, so important inside.

Witnessing

Every person you meet is an opportunity waiting to happen. We never know who will be touched by our witness unless we begin to open our mouths—your server at a restaurant, the sales clerk in a store, the guy next to you on the plane or the girl applying make-up at your Mary Kay show.

Most of us know that we are witnesses whether or not we open our mouths, but whereas we are willing to be a silent witness, we are hesitant to be verbal about our faith. Often our silent witness isn't good enough, though. Having been a non-believer, I know that they are watching Christians to see if their lifestyles match up to their profession of faith. All too often, they don't. Many a person who was watching and wondering what Christianity was all about has turned away from choosing belief because of the hypocrisy they saw displayed in the lives of believers. Christians are not perfect, but we often aren't living the Spirit-filled lives that we should be living in order to be at least a good silent witness. We need to watch our mouths and our actions. I believe that more non-Christians are turned *off* by our silent witness than they are turned onto Christ because of it.

Being ready with a spoken testimony can make the difference between a person you meet becoming a believer or remaining lost. Listening to the person you wish to witness to is the first step to building a relationship that allows you to speak your testimony. If we are not willing to listen to others, we shouldn't expect them to listen to us. Being non-judgmental and humble is mandatory in witnessing. Many, many non-believers have been turned off to Christianity because a Christian sounded "holier than thou" or pointed fingers at their lifestyles or belief systems. Pride and condemnation rarely wins converts. Caring and loving interest often does. Be prepared to share the hope you have in Jesus Christ as your loving Savior and Lord when He thrusts you into a divine appointment.

Partnership

Jesus sent His disciples out two by two. Adam had a partner—Eve. Noah didn't go into the ark alone. Paul had various people with him on his mission journeys. I had Cindy. I couldn't have done it without her.

Discipling a new believer, particularly one who's been involved in the occult, is not an easy task. It takes time, prayer, availability and even tears. With two there is strength, and Jesus promises to be in our midst. When I was being harassed or feeling inadequate in any way, inevitably Cindy was strong. When she was weak, my strengths came to the surface. We shored each other up; together we kept the dam from bursting and all the water from rushing out. As we fed ourselves on the Word, we also nourished each other. As we prayed alone in our "prayer closets," we also stormed the gates of hell together. We held each other accountable so that neither of us fell off the deep end and drowned.

I would never deal with possessed or oppressed people alone if there is any other Christian available to help me. Even though Cindy and I were occasionally alone with Tammy at the beginning of our adventure with her, we quickly learned that there was strength in partnership and began dealing with her as a pair. We were never overcome.

The Battle

We are in a war every day, but we just don't see it. The supernatural doesn't always seem real to us because we haven't the spiritual eyes to see it. But it's very real. Satan and his demons are real adversaries, and it's time to pick up our armor, put it on and prepare for the battle.

If you've never come up against the evil realm, then you are probably no threat to Satan. If you're not invading his kingdom and storming his gates, then Satan does not really need to waste his energy by harassing you. He's got you right where he wants you--inoperative, content with the status quo and probably lazy!

But if you've been harassed and fought against the demons of this world, Congratulations! You are a warrior for Christ. As warriors, we seek to advance His kingdom and seriously damage Satan's kingdom. Satan is already a defeated foe—Jesus defeated him by dying on the cross and rising from the dead—but we still need to be involved in the daily battles that come against the kingdom of heaven.

As Ephesians 6 states, our battle is "not against flesh and blood, but against...the powers of this dark world and the spiritual forces of evil in the heavenly realms," demons. Paul exhorts us to put on the full armor of God so that we can stand against the devil, our enemy. Obviously there is a battle, and God equips us so that we can fight and win. God doesn't tell us that He will take care of everything for us so that we won't have to get dirty. Instead, He gives us everything we need so that *we* can fight the battles that come our way.

Some Christians would like to exhibit their armor in a nice display cabinet—all shiny and new. No dents, no dirt, no blood. I confess that sometimes I would like my armor to stay shiny and unused also. But God has not called us to be Lay-Z-Boy warriors, shouting encouragement to those in the trenches. We are to be in the trenches with them—players, not spectators.

Other Christians are outright AWOL. Opportunity to fight is presented before them, and they turn tail and run. They don't want to fight. In fact, they are afraid to fight. Bullets fly. It's muddy. It's dangerous. Blood could flow. And they don't want it to be theirs. It's scary in the jungle. I know; I've been there. But God calls us to fight.

So we need to strap on our armor, wear it with pride and confidence in the One who gave it, and fight the battles He gives us. But don't try to fight without the full armor. Every piece is important. Your breastplate guards your heart. Without righteousness, God's righteousness, not ours, we die. Your helmet guards your head. Without salvation, we die. Your belt holds your armor together. You need the Truth as the glue to hold your faith together. Your feet need to be ready and willing to go where God calls you to go. Your shield is a movable defensive weapon that guards you against the fiery darts of the devil. It will get dented and dirty, but it will protect you. However, it's not something to hide behind; it's to be exercised. Your sword is your only offensive weapon. With the Word of God, you can deliver lethal blows to the enemy, and he will have to leave. So, be ready, be alert, be armed. You're dangerous—to Satan.

The Authority

All authority in heaven and on earth has been given to Jesus, and He gives it to us through the Holy Spirit. We have in us the authority of Jesus Christ. What an awesome power! That means that we have the authority to preach, to teach, to heal, to call out demons. Jesus did it, and so can we because He gave us the authority to do so.

When we are in the heat of battle, we have the authority to command Satan and his cohorts to "Go!" We have the authority to silence demons when they manifest in someone. We can tell them to "Be quiet!" and they will obey. We have the authority to stop a battle before it starts, to engage the enemy in battle and to win that battle. We have the authority because Jesus won the war already. We have the authority because He gave us the Holy Spirit to live within us as a powerful force—much more powerful than the enemy. Together, we can stand. Without Him, we will certainly fall.

Once I was in a class where the teacher asked us to pray for her because she was experiencing an inordinate amount of harassment in her life. I gathered with two others to do battle.

They each took a turn asking God to protect the teacher, to watch over her, be with her, help her. When it was my turn, I directly addressed the devil and in forceful terms told him to take a hike! I spoke softly, though, there's no need to yell. Afterwards, the other two stared at me as though I was an alien from Mars. They didn't know that we could speak to Satan. They didn't know that we had the authority to command him to take his grimy hands off the teacher. But we do. And we should use it. They had asked God to do the work for them, but we need to confront Satan ourselves, out loud, under the power of the blood and using the name of Jesus Christ. Jesus gave us the right, the authority and His name to do so.

Clothed with Power

I believe that the baptism with the Holy Spirit is separate from water baptism in most instances. The two can occur within an individual simultaneously, but often they do not. I believe baptism with the Holy Spirit is real—it's in the Bible (Acts 2:4, 4:31, 8:17, 9:17, 10:44-46)—and very much needed in every believer's life. We are not living the empowered Christian life that Christ wants for us without it (Acts 1:8).

Luke 11:9-13 says, "'So I say to you: Ask and it will be given to you; seek and you will find; knock and the door will be opened to you. For everyone who asks receives, he who seeks finds; and to him who knocks, the door will be opened. Which of you fathers, if your son asks for a fish, will give him a snake instead? If you then, though you are evil, know how to give good gifts to your children, how much more will your Father in heaven give the Holy Spirit to those who ask him!'"

If we are serious about being Christ-followers, then we need all the help we can get; we need the Holy Spirit to be poured out within us. Many Christians assume that they already have the Holy Spirit because He was given to dwell inside of them at their water baptism. I would agree with them—they have him. But does He have you? If you are experiencing the power of God in your life to praise Him, to teach, to heal, to cast out demons, to speak in tongues, then I would say you are baptized with the Holy Spirit. If something seems to be lacking in your spiritual life, if the Bible seems blah, worship is ho-hum and spiritual gifts are non-existent, then you need the fresh wind of the Spirit.

God our Father is willing to baptize us in the Holy Spirit, if only we would ask, seek and knock. Some people ask once and see no results and so assume it's not for them, but the Holy Spirit's power is for *every* believer. We need to go further and keep asking, move into seeking His face, His hand, and knock until He answers. And He will answer. He promised.

I believe that being filled with the Holy Spirit is not only an initial experience of Him and His power, but also an ongoing process. Because we are sinners, we continually leak and so must continually be filled back up. I am forever asking the Holy Spirit to fill me up—when I'm down, when I'm doing His work, when I need His touch, when I read His word, when I worship. I don't feel as though this is redundant or a weakness on my part, but simply it is a part of being human.

Some people are afraid of what the Holy Spirit will do if they do invite Him to fill them up to overflowing. God might cause them to speak in tongues or send them to Africa! Hallelujah! However, God will not *make* you do anything. He will call you and invite you and keep knocking on *your* door until you let him in.

Unless you yield your tongue to Him, He will not force you to speak out in tongues. You will not be out at a restaurant and ready to order your meal when out pops unintelligible words instead of the "burger" you intended to order. But if you ask the Holy Spirit for the gift of tongues and you open your mouth and make sounds, He will fill your mouth with words you've never heard before. But don't expect it to be perfectly formed right from the start. Even as you may need to work on your gift of teaching so it grows and matures, tongues may need to grow and mature also.

God also will not call you to serve Him in Africa unless you are willing to go there without coercion. He may, however, change your heart so that you do want to go to Africa or any other place outside your comfort zone. He will give you a heart for the lost and a strong desire to go wherever He wants to send you. Isn't that what we all want anyway, to be in His will?

My experience has been that through the baptism with the Holy Spirit, God has made me to be more the real *me* He intended me to be. I used to be very shy, never speaking my opinion, sometimes not even having one. But now I usually have opinions and speak out boldly on spiritual matters. I'm still shy—God didn't change my personality—but He's molded it so that I am now more of a witness for Him than ever before.

He's stretched and shaped me beyond my wildest dreams. He's brought forth in me strong desires to share the gospel, to read His word, to pray, to worship Him, to heal, to disciple. I've stepped out of my box, smashed it to bits and trod new ground.

Spiritual Gifts

I've learned a lot about spiritual gifts since I've been filled with the Holy Spirit. Paul, in 1 Corinthians 12 says that we should not be ignorant about spiritual gifts, yet many Christians still remain uninformed about them. When it came to seeking the gifts of the Spirit, I became very greedy. I make no apologies for being hungry for the things of God. I was desperate for all that God had for me. He'd placed me in a situation that was difficult to be in without the help of his gifts.

The filling or baptism of the Holy Spirit is power from on high;

spiritual gifts are the power tools we use as we walk by the Spirit. My entry gift was tongues—a gift I feel that we can all ask for and obtain. It seems to open doors into the other gifts. When we lay ourselves on His altar and give Him our whole self, God is more than willing to fill in any voids or needs we may have. While ministering to Tammy and later when persecution came from other people, the gift of tongues was a reminder to me that God was within me and still working in me and through me. What a sweet presence!

It wasn't long before other gifts came to the surface. For some reason, I felt led by God to buy books on healing. I'd never considered praying that way for people before, but now I felt God was unmistakably calling me to pray for healing. The first person I prayed for was dying of cancer. God immersed me in compassion for this woman (whom I didn't even know), and I prayed for her to be healed. She was. As I prayed for one after another, God provided many healings. Not all were healed, but enough were for me to take notice.

I began to recognize and label other gifts. Words of knowledge—knowledge God supernaturally gave me about something or someone—began to become normal for me. I believe this is a gift we all need if we are to be intercessors for others. Discernment—the ability to discern between evil spirits, the human spirit or God himself—of course, became very important in our discipling of Tammy.

One spiritual gift is not enough. Be greedy! Ask, seek and knock on His door until He opens wide His storehouse of gifts for you. He wants us to be supernatural Christians. We have a generous God, and He delights to give us all that we need to minister for His kingdom.

The Laity

I am a lay person; that means I have no "Reverend" before my name, nor do I have any kind of pastoral degree. I am simply a person who sits in the Sunday service, participates in worship and listens to a sermon. I've been involved in other activities in the church and served the Lord in many ways, but I'm no big shot in the church—just a lay person. Maybe you are too. As laity we often forget that we are important people in the body of Christ. We may think the pastor can do it all, and in fact, he should do it all. But he or she can't. God never intended for pastors to be elevated on ivory pedestals, nor did He gift them with every spiritual gift so that they can do everything without us. The fault often lies with the pastor putting himself or herself atop the pedestal, out of reach to the laity and forgetting that God's desire is for the pastor to be a humble servant like Jesus. But just as often, the fault lies with the laity thinking that pastors are trained, therefore they can and should do most of the work of the church.

When I told how my pastor and his wife acted when confronted with the possibility of table tapping and then with Tammy's seizure, I did not do it to knock them down off a pedestal and elevate Cindy. I simply told the truth. Had I been there, I may have reacted the same way. When I first saw Tammy having a seizure, I wanted to run away. But God kept me strong enough to confront evil. The pastor and his wife should not be embarrassed by their actions. God had made it clear to Cindy that it was indeed her job to cast out demons, not theirs. If He'd desired the same action from Pastor Ken and Nancy, He would have prepared *them* for the battle instead of Cindy.

Obviously God is wiser than I am and chose Cindy and I for a greater purpose. He chose ignorant lay people when he could have chosen any number of knowledgeable pastors to do the job for Him. I believe God wants to lift up lay people to their rightful place in His kingdom. Since all Christians are part of the body of Christ and no part should be exalted over another, then we should all take our place in that body. If you are a hand, be the best hand you can be. If you are a mouth, then be the best mouth you can be for the Lord. But be what you are called to be and do what you are called to do. Christianity is not a spectator sport; God gave us each spiritual gifts to be used within the body.

Occasionally, the laity outgrows the leadership in a particular church. In our case, Cindy's and mine, this eventually occurred in our church. We'd moved into the realm of the Holy Spirit, complete with the spiritual gifts He'd blessed each of us with, but we were allowed to move only so far within that particular body. Denial of Holy Spirit baptism and banning certain gifts within that church ultimately took its toll on both of our families. We are currently much happier in a church that is more charismatic in nature and freely talks about Holy Spirit baptism and spiritual gifts, wanting all to have the experiences that only the Holy Spirit can give.

Harassment

The hardest question to answer is, "Why did God allow the harassment?" At times I knew that I was totally protected from harm, and other times I had to fight against the enemy. That's life. Satan is still allowed to roam this world even though he is a defeated enemy. I learned how to stand on the authority given me by the One who defeated him and fight against him and win. I would never have learned that lesson if God had protected me from every little thing. The Word says that He won't give me more than I can handle. He has strengthened me so much through the years; I feel as though my faith is rock solid and able to take anything that is thrown my way. But when the harassment comes, I would still rather be comfortable and not have to deal with it. God and I have had many discussions over the years about just how much I can take. But I surrender to Him, for He knows best.

Watching your child go through harassment, though, is something else again. Amazingly, though, Dawn has only a vague memory of what happened to her during this time. For myself, the memory is etched deeply. It became a question of how much I trusted God. Did I trust him with my family as well as myself? How far would I follow His will for my life? Only until it became hard and uncomfortable? Or would I follow Him no matter what? I do know that God strengthened Dawn's faith through the ordeal she went through. She became a mighty warrior at the age of nine and her gift of discernment today is still very strong. Over the years as she's dealt with other problems, she's had to use that past experience of fighting in order to stay afloat.

When you ask God to strengthen your faith, watch out! He will do it, and you'll never be comfortable again. But you'll be who He wants you to be and where He wants you to be. Don't bail out when harassment comes; stand and fight.

The Occult
One Bible passage I've taught after my experience with Tammy is Deuteronomy 18:9-13.

> "When you enter the land the Lord your God is giving you, do not learn to imitate the detestable ways of the nations there. Let no one be found among you who sacrifices his son or daughter in the fire, who practices divination or sorcery, interprets omens, engages in witchcraft, or casts spells, or who is a medium or spiritist or who consults the dead. Anyone who does these things is detestable to the Lord, and because of these detestable practices the Lord your God will drive out those nations before you. You must be blameless before the Lord your God."

Tammy had been involved in all of these things and more. Her renouncing of these things took a long time. My renouncing, while shorter than hers, was also very important. I am now so sensitive to things of the occult and would no more get involved in them than I would jump off a cliff. Yet when I talk to some Christians about dabbling in the occult, they swat the idea aside that they are really caught up in anything harmful.

Some people think that they can play games like Dungeons and Dragons or Ouija Board or Tarot cards and walk away unscarred. But you can't play with Satan without getting burned. It's time we took the Deuteronomy passage seriously and become blameless before the Lord our God. Parents should pay attention to the content in TV shows, movies, music, books, computer and video games that their children watch, play, read or listen to—and also to their own entertainment choices. Books and movies that portray witchcraft as "white" magic, fun, harmless and even good are a satanic lie. Satan has a way of luring us in and desensitizing us to evil and then lowering the boom later on. You may want to cleanse your own house like I cleansed mine. Pray about it, and then do it. Satan is waiting for an open door; don't give him one.

The Things of God Versus the Things of Man

Persecution by fellow Christians is very difficult to bear. I was totally unprepared for it. I thought persecution came only by those who didn't believe in Jesus. But Jesus was persecuted by the religious authorities of His day. The early Christians were persecuted by "God-fearing" Jews as well as by unbelieving Gentiles. But somehow we think that what's printed in the Bible will never happen to us.

I think tradition often comes between God and man. Not all tradition is bad, of course, but when we begin to follow our tradition rather than the Bible or what God is doing in the church today then we allow tradition to come first in our lives. God should always come first. His word should always come first.

Coming to the Lord later in life kept me always feeling left out. I was forever playing catch-up to the traditions of the church. I hadn't memorized all the right Bible passages, prayers, hymns or liturgy. Every time I began to feel comfortable in the church, something else seemed to come up to shake me awake. There was always more to learn.

I've decided that I never want to be comfortable again—not where my faith is concerned. I'd rather be plowing new ground, ever moving towards the next step. When we begin to feel as though "we have it all," we need to watch out. If we're not growing in faith then we are stagnating and possibly rotting. The Christian walk was never meant to be easy. When we tell people that their lives will be wonderful if they'd just believe in Jesus, then we do them a disservice. Christ followers have a rocky road ahead; we don't hit the streets of gold until we die.

Meanwhile, we need to truly follow God instead of our traditions. We need to constantly be checking the Word to see if what we hear in church matches up with what God says. If it doesn't, throw it out. It's probably a bad tradition or worse—a false teaching. It is better to obey God rather than man. Obeying man may bring comfort, but it doesn't bring glory to God. Obeying God alone draws you ever closer to Him and grows you and stretches you in new ways—ways that make you uncomfortable and maybe even persecuted.

But I'd rather be as Peter and John who said to the ruler, elders and teachers of the law in Acts 4:19-20: "Judge for yourselves whether it is right in God's sight to obey you rather than God. For we cannot help speaking about what we have seen and heard."

I cannot help speaking about Jesus as Lord and Savior. I cannot help warning about our adversary, the devil. I cannot help speaking about the baptism or filling with the Holy Spirit. These topics are as important today as they were in the first Christians' lives. We still need Jesus, and we still need to be filled with his Spirit. How else can we fight our enemy?

Epilogue

Being confident of this, that he who began a good work in you will carry it on to completion until the day of Christ Jesus.
Philippians 1:6

Three years after Tammy left, I received a phone call from Nancy. Pastor Ken had taken a call at another church in the area, so I hadn't seen or heard from them for two years. Tammy had called Nancy and wanted to meet with both of them and also Cindy and I.

Tammy looked the same—only happier. Her usual grin spread wide across her face as she hugged each of us. As I studied her, she returned my look with a steady gaze of her own. She seemed self-assured and peaceful, with eyes clear and honest. This wasn't quite the same Tammy who'd left us three years ago. I was happy for her, but also sad that I'd missed the full transformation while it was in progress.

We also met her husband and her one-year-old son that day. She informed us that she was indeed a Christian as was her husband. She wanted to see us one last time before they moved away to a distant state.

She told us that she'd completed her program with Teen

Challenge in two different states despite having run away from both places. The discipline had been hard for her but also good for her—just what she'd needed. She came out of it a stronger Christian and able to stand against the enemy on her own. We asked if the seizures were gone, and she said not entirely, but they were very rare these days.

But other questions remained unanswered—Tammy was not interested in talking about the past, she was looking forward to her future. Her memory of all that had occurred during those months we'd ministered to her was hazy, and she fended off questions, saying that she was ashamed of her years of involvement in witchcraft and didn't want to talk about it. So we dropped the subject out of respect for her feelings.

She told us that she'd gone back to Wisconsin to see her family, but a total reconciliation there had not been attained. But she had seen Jan again, and even shared Jesus with her. Jan had turned her life over to Jesus and had attended Tammy's wedding.

When we left Tammy that day, Cindy and I both knew that we'd probably never see her again. She'd been ours for awhile to disciple, but now she had wings and was flying to a new home with her husband and child. We all came out winners. Tammy found Jesus and a whole new life for herself free from the bondage of the enemy.

But we also won. Because of Tammy, we both grew up in Christ and became active warriors in the Lord's army. If Tammy hadn't been open to the gospel that day, I might still be a comfortable pew-sitter—content with my level of spiritual maturity, but not really going anywhere and certainly no threat to the devil. In the close confines of my denomination and church, maybe I would have never known about the baptism with the Holy Spirit.

When anyone asks me who the one person was who most

helped me grow in my spiritual life, I tell them it was a witch. It was a witch who caused me to need Jesus like a drowning person needs a life jacket. It was a witch who brought me to my knees before God's throne where I gave myself up to Him and received back the true me He wanted me to be.

So wherever you are, Tammy, God bless you for wanting to know Jesus.

IGNITED VERSES

by Felicia Rogers

Life is poetry. Poetry is life. *Ignited Verses* is a collection of poems that contains a piece of the author's heart and soul. It is intended to ignite your passion to life and love.

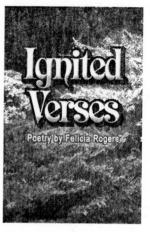

"Poeta nascitur, non fit…A poet is born, not made."

Felicia has been a poet most of her life but has taken her God-given talent more seriously the past several years.

Her poem "Sydne" appeared in poetry anthologies, *TIMELESS VOICES* and *INTERNATIONAL WHO'S WHO IN POETRY*, published in Maryland, USA, last 2006. She received an Editor's Choice Award for this poem. It is also one of the poems included in a *CD-SONGS OF POETRY* released this year by http://www.poetry.com

Paperback, 63 pages
6" x 9"
ISBN 1-4241-7974-2

About the author:

The daughter of a doctor and an insurance underwriter, she works as a nurse in a local community hospital and a nursing home.

Felicia wants to be remembered as a child of God who has learned, loved and left a legacy through ler poems.

SECRET SACRIFICES

by Cynthia Hall

Maggie Brown's ten-year-old secret is in danger of being revealed when her daughter Tracey is abducted. Desperate to find her, Maggie contacts Tracey's biological father, Matt Sanford. The unsuspecting father uses his law enforcement skills as he would with any routine kidnaping case to help locate Tracey. Maggie and Matt rush against time and a powerful tropical storm to get to Tracey before she is taken away forever. While Maggie and Matt's undercover journey leads them into dangerous twists and turns involving a devious Caribbean kidnaping ring and a bad cop, Tracey is fighting her own battle when she is brought into a questionable environment of abuse and uncertainty. Maggie's frantic search forces her to make decisions that could shake the stability of her private world. Tracey is faced with finding strength beyond her comprehension, and Matt must decide if he is able to forgive.

Paperback, 195pages
6" x 9"
ISBN 1-4241-7257-8

About the author:

When Cynthia L. Hall began work on her debut novel, *Secret Sacrifices*, she worked for a local sheriff's department, which gave her great insight into law enforcement and helped with the details. Cynthia's writing includes human interest stories and freelance photojournalism. She and her husband live in Ohio. They have one daughter.

LORD OF ALL SCIENCE
ESSAYS FOR GOOD
by Ralph Fudge

Lord of All Science is a collection of fourteen essays that have the purpose of doing good by first pointing out why the author believes in God as a result of studying science, and second, by offering knowledge and ideas collected over his lifetime. The first chapter asks the question, "Does God Exist?" and discusses solid reasons for believing that He does. The next three chapters point out how the great order found in nature and the extreme complexity of life both support the belief that God exists. The remaining ten chapters discuss ideas such as thinking, knowledge, wisdom, and education, as well as good and evil, human nature, the benefits of work, human weight control, and finally, happiness through the development of good relationships with family and friends. A lot of Christian doctrine is presented and discussed. The book was written at the suggestion of the author's friends.

Paperback, 177 pages
5.5" x 8.5"
ISBN 1-4241-5028-0

About the author:

Ralph Fudge was born in the small town of Blakely, Georgia. He has been married 38 years and has two children and a grandson. Ralph has been a teacher of high school and college science courses for 33 years and is active in his church in Thomasville, Georgia.

LIFE-CHANGING MESSAGES
WITH ETERNAL DIVIDENDS

by Tonya Fleming

Who is this God that many speak about, and where did he come from? God's Maker was a four-letter word. In other words God was formed by one word, and the word is love. His Maker from the beginning of time declared God's creation. This word has more power and life than any other word. This word formed an everlasting Spirit, the Spirit of God. The billion-dollar question has been answered. Where did God come from? When these four letters connected, it brought forth so much power that it created God. God's creator lives on the inside of him. God's in love! And he's in love with you.

Paperback, 48 pages
6" x 9"
ISBN 1-60474-559-2

About the author:

Tonya L. Fleming was born December 14, 1963, in Bellville, Texas. She is a graduate of Temple High School, better known as Tonya Shaw. Fleming is seeking an associate's degree in communications and a master's degree in English at the University of Phoenix. She is an author, a preacher of righteousness, a wife and a mother of two. Fleming is the founder of House of Compassion ministries. She is an intercessor. In other words, she stands in the gap between God and man praying for souls to be saved and people to be delivered from burdens and yokes that are destroying their lives. Look for *Messages from Your First Love* coming soon.